*How To Start a Business
and Be Your Own Boss*

MID-CAREER ENTREPRENEUR

JOSEPH R. MANCUSO

Enterprise · Dearborn
a division of Dearborn Publishing Group, Inc.

While a great deal of care has been taken to provide accurate and current information, the ideas, suggestions, general principles and conclusions presented in this text are subject to local, state and federal laws and regulations, court cases and any revisions of same. The reader is thus urged to consult legal counsel regarding any points of law—this publication should not be used as a substitute for competent legal advice.

Publisher: Kathleen A. Welton
Associate Editor: Karen A. Christensen
Editorial Assistant: Kristen Landreth
Senior Project Editor: Jack L. Kiburz
Interior Design: Lucy Jenkins
Cover Design: Design Alliance, Inc.
Copyeditor: Patricia A. Stahl

Published by Enterprise • Dearborn,
a division of Dearborn Publishing Group, Inc.

Printed in the United States of America

93 94 95 10 9 8 7 6 5 4 3 2 1

Library of Congress Cataloging-in-Publication Data

Mancuso, Joseph
    The mid-career entrepreneur: how to start a business and be your
own boss / Joseph R. Mancuso.
       p.   cm.
    Includes index.
    ISBN 0-79310-719-9 (pbk.)
    1. New business enterprises—United States. 2. Entrepreneurship—
United States. 3. Self-employed—United States. I. Title.
HD62.5.M355   1994
658'.041—dc20   93-28991
                                              CIP

Contents

List of Figures

■ ■

Introduction

"If you give a person a fish you feed him for a day. If you teach him to fish, you feed him for a lifetime."

This is a special book written for a broad general purpose. The American economy has experienced such dramatic change during the last few years that a new breed of mid-career executive/entrepreneur has emerged. It used to be that most small business owners were people who spent their entire careers in small businesses.

After finishing their schooling, they began in a small business and then worked for one small business after another during their careers. They did this because it was very difficult to start, say at the age of 40, as a lower-level executive at a major U.S. corporation. People who started at IBM or GE right out of school would have a 20-year lead time and know much more about the company and its operations. But remember, for every action there's an opposite but equal reaction. So, while the above is still true, the U.S. job market has been a disaster. Some say one in eight people is either unemployed or underemployed.

Even with the U.S. economy in the doldrums for the last five years, it's been commonplace for the first 20 years of someone's career to be paid for and developed by large Fortune 500 companies. But today, thousands of people are being laid off by the large Fortune 500 companies at mid-career. This has created an unparalleled crisis within the U.S. economy.

The Chinese symbol for crisis combines the two symbols for opportunity and danger. What are these mid-career people to do? They're not in a good position to switch to another large company because the new company is also probably downsizing. And before they hire from the outside, they tend to promote from within wherever possible. Consequently, many mid-career executives are opting to operate their own businesses. They have found opportunity within the danger of unemployment.

The motivating reason is they want to have the independence of being their own boss. The bureaucratic baloney and the politics have worn down their need to achieve, and they wonder if dedicating their entire career to a large, unfeeling corporation is really worth the retirement party or the gold watch. These people don't have a strong personal desire to start a business. They don't have a burning cause or issue. Fundamentally, they are seeking independence. This book is written to serve them. There are many paths that eventually lead to running your own business, so I caution you to be alert to the "catch 22" implied by this old saying: "Many are stubborn in pursuit of the path they choose, not in the goal they seek."

Here are your choices: First, you can start your own business. (It's very hard to start your own business, and it's not often done by mid-career executives.) It usually takes longer than buying an existing business, but it usually costs less. Second, you could acquire a franchise. This is a very popular choice for mid-career executives because they possess some capital and some expertise. (See Chapter 4 on franchising.) The third choice is to acquire a business someone else has already started. Again, this is a very popular choice—almost equal in popularity to franchising. (See Chapter 5 on how to create a deal flow.)

A fourth choice is partnering, where you become an investor and small stockholder with minority interest in someone else's business. I don't highlight this option in any one chapter of this book because I assume that you're more interested in succeeding in your primary mission of total independence. Partnering, especially a minority interest in a small business, gives you is nothing more than what you had at your large company job. In fact, it is usually less attractive because you're under the dominance of one individual, usually an entrepreneur, and that can be much worse than being under the dominance of a corporate structure.

■ The Entrepreneurial Process

Entrepreneurship is the ultimate aphrodisiac. It gets you to believe that you're bigger and better than you usually are. When your shop is really humming and business is flowing through the doors, the adrenaline flow is greater than for athletes. You can try drugs and alcohol, but you will discover they have only short-term effects.

In my experience in working with entrepreneurs, the longest sustained high I've ever seen comes from within people who are running their own businesses. Entrepreneurs who have achieved some level of success are adrenaline factories who pump out hope, happiness and are in a constant state of euphoria.

If I gave one piece of advice in this introduction it would be summed up in the slogan of the nonprofit membership association called the Center for Entrepreneurial Management Inc. and the Chief Executive Officers Club (CEM & CEO). I started both these groups in 1978 after I left the faculty of Worcester Polytechnic Institute (WPI) in Massachusetts as chairman of the management department.

At that time I thought entrepreneurs and independent business people should be linked together in some educational way for mutual benefit. After all, peers exchanging ideas has the greatest impact for changing behaviors. The mission statement for my organization says: *"We are a nonprofit membership association of CEOs and entrepreneurs dedicated to improving the quality and profitability of our enterprises through shared experience and personal growth."*

But that's a bit of a mouthful, so I began the association on this slogan, which is repeated today on all our invoices. *"It's O.K. to be independent, but there is no reason to be alone."* If you are browsing this book in a bookstore and you don't buy it, at least accept this one piece of advice: **"Don't do it alone!"**

In building your business, be sure that you include others from whom you can accept advice. No person is an island. Our associations' success proves the benefit of CEOs and entrepreneurs exchanging ideas. Very few things that you will encounter in your business have not already been encountered by someone else running a similar business. You can either make all the mistakes that others have made or you can profit by others' mistakes and run your business more effectively.

The odds of succeeding in a new business are very small. Those who have succeeded are able to seek outside help and guidance. They are not smarter. They are not better processors of information. They are not taller or better looking. They are not richer. They all are good listeners who can profit by hearing how others have done it. They are seldom inventive in what they do; they are more like applied engineers who find techniques and ideas that others have found successful and apply them to their case.

I strongly suggest you get involved in some local activity that will put you into a sharing mode with other CEOs and entrepreneurs to significantly increase both the fulfillment of running your own business and the likelihood that your business will succeed. The chamber of commerce, the CEO Clubs, the Young Presidents Organization (YPO), The Executive Committee (TEC), regional small business associations and CEO divisions of large trade organizations are well worth the price of membership. I also suggest reading my other book, *Mancuso's Small Business Resource Guide 1990* (Simon & Schuster) for my recommendations and an annotated bibliography of resources. And remember the Entrepreneur's Puzzle: "Either I am an entrepreneur or I'm unemployed."

■ ■

PART ONE

■

The Mid-Career Decision

■ ■ ■ ■ ■ ■ ■ ■ ■ ■ ■ ■ ■ ■ ■ ■ ■ ■ ■ ■

1

Are You a Mid-Career Entrepreneur?

People who create an ongoing enterprise out of nothing are generally called entrepreneurs. Entrepreneurs do not normally appear later in life. Most begin their businesses when they finish formal schooling. Of course, the popular exceptions are Ray Kroc and Colonel Harlan Sanders, who founded McDonald's and Kentucky Fried Chicken, respectively, when they were approaching retirement age. The father of the conglomerate, the late Royal Little, didn't start Textron's acquisition binge until he was 57 years old, and P.T. Barnum didn't get involved with the circus until the age of 60, when he also remarried. But these are colorful exceptions.

My association, CEM,* has published research about entrepreneurs for three decades. I like to refer to them with a three-word phrase—Ready, Fire, Aim! So far, I have sold 14,000 T-shirts emblazoned with these words.

My slogan puts entrepreneurs into perspective, but it does little to explain how they get that way in the first place. That's a puzzling issue with no once-and-for-all answer. Although clues exist to explain their behavior, no irrefutable causal relationship has been established. A knowledge of their early development gives us a better window into their motivations and behavior. The traits I'm about to describe apply to all entrepreneurs, including those who

---

*The Center for Entrepreneurial Management, Inc., founded in 1978. CEM is the world's largest nonprofit association of entrepreneurial managers, with more than 3,000 members.

emerge late in life. If you fit the profile, you're home free. But even if you don't, bucking the odds is an entrepreneurial trait.

■ The Early Development of Entrepreneurs

Most entrepreneurs enjoy talking about their childhood. And most of the time, their recollections are fascinating. They were interesting and unusual children. It is during childhood that entrepreneurial tendencies first show themselves: As early as age four or five, entrepreneurs-to-be are peddling lemonade on the sidewalk at a penny a glass. At eight or nine, they're delivering newspapers to earn money for a new bike. In their early teens they're collecting coins, rocks, stamps or photographs. These activities may be fun, but they are always aimed toward profit and growth. By the time they reach high school they may actually be running their own businesses on a small scale. In short, most entrepreneurs were enterprising children.

The Firstborn

The firstborn child is the most likely to become an entrepreneur. Firstborns are overrepresented in *Who's Who*, and they dominate most achievement rankings in U.S. culture. George Washington, Abraham Lincoln, Thomas Jefferson, Woodrow Wilson, Franklin D. Roosevelt—all were firstborn children. Of the first 23 astronauts to go on U.S. space missions, 21 were either the eldest or only children. This is remarkable when you consider that later-born children outnumber firstborns by two to one in the general U.S. population. In a recent analysis of 1,618 Merit Scholarship winners, 971 were firstborn children.* My association, CEM, has 3,000 dues-paying members ($96 annually), and my research says 2,000 of them are firstborns. Statistically, just over 1,000 should be firstborns.

Firstborns are most likely to accept their parents' standards, to be traditionally oriented and to call themselves religious. It's the later-born children who are likely to rebel.

I have no data on second and middle children, but I enjoy watching someone's face light up when I announce that second children tend to be lawyers. They have to deal with an older, more powerful sibling by using legal tactics ("I'll tell Mom") and persuasive maneuvers, not including force. They go through life cleaning up the messes created by their older siblings.

---

*D. McClelland, *The Achieving Society* (New York: Van Nostrand, 1961).

Relationship with Income-Producing Parent

The entrepreneur's obsessive need to achieve may often be traced to his or her relationship with the income-producing parent, most often the father. If they have a good relationship, even if Dad was not a great success, the son or daughter strives to make him proud. Dad's subtlest signs of approval, such as a nod or a half-smile, are the child's most cherished rewards. A surprisingly large number of entrepreneurs are the offspring of self-employed fathers. Thus, the free spirit and independence of self-employment are molded into many young entrepreneurs-to-be and can never be totally suppressed even in their later careers.

In cases where the father-son relationship is less cordial—even strained—the son may try to achieve a greater level of success than the father in order to prove he's the better man. Finally, if the father was not present during the entrepreneur's childhood—because of death, divorce or desertion—the son may have been forced to assume the provider's role in the family. Inheriting a great deal of responsibility at an early age can promote maturity and, with it, entrepreneurial tendencies. Very seldom does the male entrepreneur have an "average," subdued Oedipal relationship with his father.

The Home Environment

Recently, a friend called me from Wichita, Kansas, and asked me to counsel a 19-year-old boy who was a family friend. His parents were prominent entrepreneurs in town, and they were desperate to help their only child. He was failing in school and in sports, and he seemed to have no purpose in life.

I don't do this sort of work often (I usually get paid), but these entrepreneurs had been CEM members for almost a dozen years and prevailed on me through a mutual friend. I never met the parents. Tom was impressed with our offices, which offered panoramic views of Manhattan. He had read several of my books and tapes years ago and was anxious to meet me. We got off to a good visit.

He was tall and a good basketball player, but even this sport had suffered from what was described as "his problem."

I spent half a day with him and uncovered the underlying issue. His parents divorced when he was seven, and over the next four years he lived with one, then the other, and then with both sets of grandparents.

Because his parents were successful entrepreneurs in business together, they remained business partners after the divorce. As luck would have it, they eventually remarried and Tom returned to the family home as he was entering puberty.

Tom tightened up when he said they divorced a second time and recalled how the story had been pretty big news in Kansas. He shook his head and said, "Everybody in Topeka knew about the comedy."

Today, his folks are still business partners, but each is married to someone else. In New York, it may not be as strange as the Woody Allen/Mia Farrow saga, but in Kansas it was pretty big news. Tom reasoned that his grades in school and his inability to "put the ball in the hole" were directly related to his "problem." I first thought his troubles were from drugs or a girlfriend, but I could see he wanted sympathy for his confused upbringing. Everyone else had always responded with, "Oh, you poor boy," and the real culprits were the two sets of grandparents who continued to echo the "poor boy" chant.

I don't know what prompted my response, but it came spontaneously. I said, "You lucky kid, you could be on your way to becoming a great person. Did you know that most of the great people in history had screwed-up childhoods? Abraham Lincoln's mother was sent to a mental hospital, and Winston Churchill's should have been." Then I mentioned Picasso, Rembrandt, Matisse and a few other artists. It was even more pronounced in their cases, I told him.

I don't know if the above is true or not, but I concluded with a topic I actually had some data about, and I made it all sound true:

"Did you know that Ted Turner's dad committed suicide?" I asked. "It was pretty messy—shot himself in the head. Did you know that a high percentage of famous entrepreneurs had devastating fights with one or both of their parents, or that many were created by fathers who deserted the family? The young child had to produce or die. Almost all high achievers are produced by mixed-up childhoods."

I got up from my desk and brought him over to the telescope, which was fixed not on the twin towers of the 207-story World Trade Center, but on the Manhattan General Post Office.

I had him look through the scope while I continued the monologue: "If you want a career at the post office, you need a nice, balanced childhood. If you don't believe me, walk over there and ask the thousands of employees a little about their backgrounds. I'll bet you not one of them is an offspring of an entrepreneurial couple who were married and divorced twice."

Finally, I got a positive nod from Tom. My message had reached the back of the brain.

I concluded with my favorite truism: Do you know what happens to the A students in college? They go on to be college professors. The B students, who were not quite as bright but outperformed the majority of the class, are the single biggest group of college graduates. They end up working for the C students. The rest of them, the ones who flunk out or quit school, they become the movie stars, the athletes or the entrepreneurs."

After he left my office, I turned to my wife, Karla, and said what was really on my mind: "Boy, you should have met this sweet, naive kid from the Midwest. He has had it tough. His mom and dad are well-known entrepreneurs who married and divorced each other not once, but twice. The poor kid is confused and lost. I can't blame him because his folks were more immature than he. I doubt whether I'd have made much of my life if I had come from that environment."

As a footnote to this story, I heard from our mutual friend that Tom has started a business and plans to be married later this year. I think I got to him.

The foregoing comments have been offered as insight into the question: What makes entrepreneurs tick? Why are they more at home in their swivel chairs than in their living rooms? What makes them willing to lose their spouses, their wits and even their wads—not once, but three or four times? Why can't they be happy working for someone else? Why do they always have to go it alone? When other kids were out playing, why were they busy hustling lemonade? When their friends were dating cheerleaders or football heroes, why were they organizing rock concerts? Or marketing grandmother's pickle recipe? Or inventing a better fly swatter? Are they smarter than the rest of us—or just crazy?

■ Measuring Your Entrepreneurial Potential

The quizzes in Figures 1.1 and 1.2 are designed to help you gauge your potential for success as an entrepreneur. In the first quiz, you will be trying to determine whether you have the basic mind-set of an entrepreneur; in the second, you will analyze your sources of motivation. There are no right or wrong answers, per se, so don't try to second-guess the questions. The important thing is to be honest about yourself. With that in mind, let's begin.

Figure 1.1   Entrepreneurial Personality Profile

Under each question, check the answer that comes closest to the way you feel.

1. Are you a self-starter?

   a. I do things on my own. Nobody has to tell me to get going.
   b. If someone gets me started, I keep going all right.
   c. Easy does it. I don't put myself out until I have to.

2. How do you feel about other people?

   a. I like people. I can get along with just about anybody.
   b. I have plenty of friends—I don't need anyone else.
   c. Most people bug me.

3. Can you lead others?

   a. I can get most people to go along when I start something.
   b. I can give the orders if someone tells me what we should do.
   c. I let someone else get things moving. Then I go along if I feel like it.

4. Can you take responsibility?

   a. I like to take charge of things and see them through.
   b. I'll take over if I have to, but I'd rather let someone else be responsible.
   c. There's always some eager beaver around wanting to show how smart he is. I say let him.

5. How good an organizer are you?

   a. I like to have a plan before I start. I'm usually the one to get things lined up when the gang wants to do something.
   b. I do all right unless things get too goofed up. Then I cop out.
   c. You get all set and then something comes along and blows the whole bag. So I just take things as they come.

6. How good a worker are you?

   a. I can keep going as long as I need to. I don't mind working hard for something I want.
   b. I'll work hard for a while, but when I've had enough, that's it, man!
   c. I can't see that hard works gets you anywhere.

7. Can you make decisions?

   a. I can make up my mind in a hurry if I have to. It usually turns out O.K., too.
   b. I can if I have plenty of time. If I have to make up my mind fast, I think later I should have decided the other way.
   c. I don't like to be the one who has to decide things. I'd probably blow it.

8. Can people trust what you say?

   a. You bet they can. I don't say things I don't mean.
   b. I try to be on the level most of the time, but sometimes I just say what's easiest.
   c. What's the sweat if the other person doesn't know the difference?

9. Can you stick with it?

   a. If I make up my mind to do something, I don't let anything stop me.
   b. I usually finish what I start—if it doesn't get fouled up.
   c. If it doesn't go right away, I turn off. Why beat your brains out?

10. How good is your health?

   a. I never run down.
   b. I have enough energy for most things I want to do.
   c. I run out of gas sooner than most of my friends.

   Now tally your answers. If most of your checks are beside the *a* responses, you probably have what it takes to run a business. If not, you're likely to have more trouble than you can handle by yourself. You'd better find a partner who is strong in your weak areas. If most of your responses were *c*, not even a good partner will be able to shore you up.

Figure 1.2 Entrepreneurial Motivation Assessment

Answer the following questions as objectively as possible in order to understand your motivations to become an entrepreneur. If you strongly agree with a statement, score it a 7; if you strongly disagree, score it a 1; if you are in the middle, score it a 4.

Agree   Disagree
7 6 5 4 3 2 1

1. I love to be with people I like even when it serves no purpose. ☐ ☐ ☐ ☐ ☐ ☐ ☐

2. In many situations, clarifying who is in charge is the most important business at hand. ☐ ☐ ☐ ☐ ☐ ☐ ☐

3. When playing a game, I am as concerned with how well I play in my own estimation as I am with whether or not I win. ☐ ☐ ☐ ☐ ☐ ☐ ☐

4. I believe it is most important to have the respect of others in your community. ☐ ☐ ☐ ☐ ☐ ☐ ☐

5. When I set a goal, there is a good chance I will make it even though it doesn't always happen. ☐ ☐ ☐ ☐ ☐ ☐ ☐

6. It is important to have possessions that will influence others to respect me. ☐ ☐ ☐ ☐ ☐ ☐ ☐

7. Losing a friend is very upsetting to me. I work hard to regain friends I have lost. ☐ ☐ ☐ ☐ ☐ ☐ ☐

8. I insist on the respect of people under me, even if I have to push them around a bit to get it. ☐ ☐ ☐ ☐ ☐ ☐ ☐

9. I need lots of warmth from others, and I give it back. ☐ ☐ ☐ ☐ ☐ ☐ ☐

10. I think about how what I am doing today will affect my future five years from now. ☐ ☐ ☐ ☐ ☐ ☐ ☐

11. I like to set up measures of how well I am progressing. ☐ ☐ ☐ ☐ ☐ ☐ ☐

12. I am very concerned with the efficiency and quality of my work. ☐ ☐ ☐ ☐ ☐ ☐ ☐

	Agree						Disagree
	7	6	5	4	3	2	1

13. Many people need advice and help, and someone should give it to them whether they want it or not. □ □ □ □ □ □ □

14. Strong actions are needed when people make mistakes. □ □ □ □ □ □ □

15. I enjoy social get-togethers and make time to go to them. □ □ □ □ □ □ □

16. A key purpose in my life is to do things that have not been done before. □ □ □ □ □ □ □

17. If I move to a new area, I imagine the first thing I would do is develop new friends. Without close friends, I'm like a plant without water. □ □ □ □ □ □ □

18. I need to get strong emotional reactions out of others because then I know I'm getting somewhere. □ □ □ □ □ □ □

19. I need very much to be liked by others. □ □ □ □ □ □ □

20. My friends may sometimes think it dull, but I find myself talking about how to overcome future obstacles I have anticipated. □ □ □ □ □ □ □

21. My close relationships are very valuable to me. □ □ □ □ □ □ □

22. My reason for being in business is to become rich, rich, rich! □ □ □ □ □ □ □

23. I don't like working on a project without knowing how well I'm doing, so I make plans that allow me to measure how fast I'm proceeding toward my goals. □ □ □ □ □ □ □

24. I like to get involved in community activities because it gives me a chance to have influence where I live. □ □ □ □ □ □ □

25. The real meaning of life is the personal relationships we form. □ □ □ □ □ □ □

Figure 1.2 (continued)

	Agree						Disagree
	7	6	5	4	3	2	1

26. I do best when I have some room to choose my own goals.   □ □ □ □ □ □ □

27. If people don't know you really appreciate them, you can't expect them to do a good job,   □ □ □ □ □ □ □

28. In everything I do—work, sports, hobbies—I try to set high standards for myself; otherwise where's the fun of it?   □ □ □ □ □ □ □

29. It's people that make up a business, not a lot of stock piled up on the shelves.   □ □ □ □ □ □ □

30. I always thought I would enjoy being a famous politician, actor or athlete and live in the lap of luxury.   □ □ □ □ □ □ □

These 30 questions can be subdivided into three groups: achievement, affiliation and power. Total your score in each group to understand your personal sources of motivation.

Achievement

Question #	Your Score
3	_____
5	_____
10	_____
11	_____
12	_____
16	_____
20	_____
23	_____
26	_____
28	_____
Total	_____

Affiliation

Question #	Your Score
1	_____
7	_____
9	_____
15	_____
17	_____
19	_____
21	_____
25	_____
27	_____
29	_____
Total	_____

Power

Question #	Your Score
2	_____
4	_____
6	_____
8	_____
13	_____
14	_____
18	_____
22	_____
24	_____
30	_____
Total	_____

After totaling each category, plot your scores on Figure 1.3.

Figure 1.3 Individual Motive Profile

High—50—			
Mod-High—35—			
Moderate—25—			
Mod-Low—12.5—			
Low—0—			
	Achievement	Affiliation	Power

■ Understanding the Sources of Motivation

The three categories of achievement, affiliation and power are based upon studies of motivation done by Dr. David C. McClelland of Harvard University. Let's take a closer look at these basic needs in relation to entrepreneurship.

Achievement and Entrepreneurship

The need for *achievement* directs a person's attention to getting the job done, toward the achievement of his or her goals. The goals may be competitive, but the focus is on doing well, not on beating others. Or the goal may be relatively noncompetitive, like accomplishing something unique that has never been done before. Whatever the goal, the achievement orientation focuses on getting to it, not on relationships with other people involved.

A high level of achievement motivation is often used to explain some important aspects of entrepreneurial behavior, including:

- setting and competing against self-imposed standards
- setting moderate risk goals
- seeking feedback and learning from it

These are the outward behaviors of someone who is inwardly hard-driving, competitive, goal-oriented and highly committed.

Although this high level of achievement motivation can be a great asset to the prospective entrepreneur, it can also be a drawback to certain role demands.

- Extreme independence and self-reliance can be an obstacle to seeking outside assistance and to developing good team relations.

- High personal standards can make you intolerant of others who cannot meet your expectations, and this can inhibit team building.
- Extreme self-reliance, self-confidence and a doer orientation tend to be an obstacle to delegation of authority. This imposes upper limits on how much you can effectively organize and thus on how big your business can become.

Affiliation and Entrepreneurship

The need for *affiliation* is a desire to be close to people, to enjoy warm friendships and to build good relationships. It often links up with achievement as a powerful means of reaching goals—through interaction and cooperation.

While considerably less researched than the achievement motive, there is evidence that this motive can be crucial in the early stages of a venture.

If coupled with a high level of achievement motivation, affiliation can be a valuable lubricant for team and interpersonal relationships. Most entrepreneurs who have been through a business start-up know that during this early stage, survival is a predominant issue. In the heat of start-up, relationships often take a back seat to sales, deliveries and cash flow. Yet we know that unresolved conflicts among team members can lead to serious, costly crises or even failure of a business. Given these common start-up pressures, a moderate to high level of affiliation motivation can be an important asset for an entrepreneur. This type of person makes interpersonal issues a more legitimate priority and finds it more natural to deal with them because it meets an internal psychological need.

On the other hand, certain aspects of affiliation motivation can contribute to avoidance of conflicts and confrontations, and therefore retard goal orientation.

Power and Entrepreneurship

The need for *power* is the need to dominate or influence other people. It is not just a need to be on top. The need to convince others of your opinions or to cause them to experience strong emotions is also need for influence.

The need for power can be potentially destructive in building a substantial enterprise. Ironically, data collected previously by McClelland indicated that when coupled with a high achievement need, high power motivation was a common motivational characteristic of top-level U.S. corporate executives and presidents.

High achievement motivation alone is not enough for success in a large corporation. The complexity of large organizations, the more politicized nature of their reward and status systems and the power inherent in their economic roles can amply satisfy high needs for power. People without those power needs are likely to find fewer inherent opportunities for need satisfaction and may find pure achievement needs unrewarded or occasionally punished as boat-rocking or overambition.

Our contention here is that beyond the single proprietorship, a strong need for power contains many seeds of self-destruction because it inhibits the forming of an entrepreneurial team to launch and build a substantial business. Some manifestations of the power motive are:

- clashes over authority, prerogatives and control, rather than over how to solve problems or attain goals
- emphasis on gain, personal status, influence and reputation rather than on tasks and goals
- interpersonal clashes perceived as unsolvable personality conflicts
- emphasis on status symbols—salary, titles, stock ownership, office location and space, company automobiles, etc.
- emphasis on getting rich quick rather than on building a substantial business

Changing Motivation

Implicit in our definition of motives as "an habitual pattern of thinking with feelings and values attached" or "a recurrent concern with certain goals" is the recipe for changing or increasing one's motivation. If motives are but a habitual pattern of thought, all you need to do is think differently and your motivation will change.

How do you learn to think differently in key situations in your life? McClelland, in his classic paper, "Towards a Theory of Motive Acquisition," suggests a four-pronged approach:

1. *Self-assessment.* You first need to be aware of how you naturally tend to perceive the people and situations you encounter. Try to understand your present motivation—and its consequences.
2. *Practice.* You next need to learn the elements (or subcategories) of the motives you want to increase, and practice thinking about situations in terms of the new motive over and over again until this new pattern of thought becomes habitual.

3. *Goal-setting.* Set goals, solve problems, plan and act in ways that are consistent with your new perspective.

4. *Reinforcement.* Finally, you can put yourself in situations and choose to be with people who can give you feedback on, stimulate and generally support your new way of thinking and behaving.

These inputs act together to create a positive feedback loop that can continually reinforce the new motive you are trying to learn. The process of change consists of consciously effecting the steps in the familiar motivational paradigm:

MOTIVES———BEHAVIOR———RESULTS IN LIFE

Let's see what happens at each step.

Step 1. Understand your natural unconscious motives—the ways you instinctively see and think about people and situations. Then think about the motive you want to develop and strategize how to deal with situations and people in a new way. If you are working on developing your power motivation, fantasize how you will argue assertively for your position at the next meeting you attend. This can be a rehearsal for action.

Step 2. Behave in a way consistent with the new motives. Try a new way of dealing with people or situations.

Step 3. Monitor your results in life. What is the impact of thinking in power terms and acting in powerful ways? This feedback is crucial in helping you develop a new pattern of motivated thought and perfect the behavioral and interpersonal skills that go with it.

As you continue to practice seeing, thinking, acting, putting yourself in situations and getting results consistent with the new motive, you will find it becomes more natural—a new instinctive, automatic or "unconscious" way of reacting to people and situations. At this point, your underlying motives can truly be said to have changed. But it should again be emphasized: All you really need to do to change your motives is to think differently.

2

The Mid-Career Entrepreneur's Quiz

Who is the entrepreneur? What molds her and what motivates him? How does he differ from the nine-to-fiver, and where are those differences most telling? Why will one brother set out to build a business, while another aspires to promotions and perks? Why does one stay up nights working on a business plan, while the other brags about his pension plan? Is it brains or luck? Is it hard work, or does it just happen?

When most people think of entrepreneurs, names like Ross Perot, Ted Turner, Henry Ford, Edwin Land or even Famous (Wally) Amos automatically come to mind. But in fact, American entrepreneurs number in the millions. Of the 15 million businesses in this country, more than 11 million are operated as sole proprietorships. Although not all of these businesses can be labeled "entrepreneurial ventures," the dictionary definition of an entrepreneur is "one who manages, organizes and assumes the risk of a business or enterprise."

Why then do we think of the entrepreneur in almost mythical terms? The answer is easy. Like the cowboys of the old American West, the entrepreneur represents freedom: freedom from the boss, freedom from the time clock and, with a lot of hard work and more than a little luck, freedom from the bank. This freedom issue is at the heart of why so many people choose to launch a business at mid-career. They do so because they seek freedom.

Entrepreneurs are the backbone of the free enterprise system. When an entrepreneur gambles on his or her skills and abilities, everyone stands to win. Innovative products and services created by entrepreneurs constantly revitalize the marketplace and create thousands of new jobs in the process. One need look no further than the light bulb, the automobile or, most recently, the personal computer to see how entrepreneurs can change the country's way of life. What's more, nothing keeps a big corporation on its toes like an entrepreneur nipping at its heels—and its markets.

So who is the entrepreneur? Anyone who has ever looked at a problem and seen an opportunity, as well as a solution, is a likely prospect. The same goes for anyone who feels his or her ambition is being held in check by corporate red tape. But then it takes more than just cleverness and frustration to get an entrepreneurial venture off the ground. It takes guts, an indefatigable personality and total dedication to a dream. On top of that, it takes the kind of person who can call working 90 hours a week fun.

While there is no single entrepreneurial archetype, there are certain traits that indicate an entrepreneurial personality. They are summed up in the following story.

■ The Entrepreneurial Rooster

A farmer's chickens stopped laying eggs, so he "fired" all his roosters. He went to market to get a new bunch, and while he was looking around he was approached by a short, suspicious-looking fellow who said: "I hear you're looking for about 40 new roosters, but I think you're crazy because it just so happens that I've got a real deal for you. Over here in the corner I've got a skinny little 'entrepreneurial' rooster. He can keep your whole hen house happy, and they'll soon be laying eggs again."

The farmer just laughed. "A rooster *that* size? Do you know how many hens I have?" But when the man offered him a 30-day, money-back guarantee, he figured he couldn't go wrong and decided to give the rooster a tryout.

After a few days, the farmer discovered that his hens were smiling, happy and laying eggs. After about the tenth day, the farmer saw that his ducks, who lived next door to the chicken coop, were *also* smiling, happy and laying eggs.

A few days after that, the farmer noticed that his eight-foot-tall pet ostrich was *also* smiling, happy and laying eggs. Then, about a week later, the farmer noticed that his cows were giving twice as much milk as they used to. The farmer couldn't believe it—this skinny little rooster was single-handedly saving his farm from bankruptcy.

However, remembering his 30-day guarantee, the farmer kept his eye on the rooster, just in case. On the morning of the 29th day, he looked out from his bedroom window, but he couldn't locate the rooster. He went outside and looked around, but it was nowhere in sight. Then, far off in the desert, the farmer saw a black cloud. He hopped into his pickup truck and drove off in that direction. When he got nearer, he saw that the black cloud was actually a flock of vultures circling a limp form lying on the ground. "I *knew* he couldn't keep up that pace," the farmer thought. There the rooster lay, his tongue out and his head to one side; he was dead as a doornail.

The farmer felt that the rooster's death was a tragedy, a waste of an unusual kind of drive and spirit. But he also remembered that he could collect on the guarantee because the rooster was not going to be able to perform on the 30th day. He went over to pick up the rooster and take him back to the farm. Just as he reached down, the rooster turned his head, pecked the farmer on the hand and said, "Cut it out and take a walk—this is the only way I can get those vultures!"

This story sums up the totality of the entrepreneurial personality. The following quiz, developed from a series of questionnaire analyses performed by the Center for Entrepreneurial Management, will help you dissect the personality into its key components (see Figure 2.1). The quiz has been updated every five years since it was originally published. Versions have appeared in *Playboy* and *Penthouse* magazines. So if you've ever wondered if you have what it takes to be an entrepreneur, here is your chance to find out.

■ Answers to the Quiz

1. The independent way of life is not so much genetic as it is learned, and the first school for any entrepreneur is the home. So it's only natural that a child who has grown up in a home where at least one parent is self-employed is more likely to try her hand at her own business than a child whose parents were in the civil service. My own research has shown this to be the case more than two-thirds of the time. Some good examples of this are Fred Smith of Federal Express, Howard Hughes of Hughes Tool and New York real estate tycoon Donald Trump, all of whom parlayed modest family businesses into major fortunes.

2. This question is tricky because the independent-minded entrepreneur will often quit a job instead of waiting around to get fired. However, the dynamics of the situation are the same; the impasse results from the entrepreneur's brashness and almost compulsive need to be right. Steven Jobs and Steven Wozniak went ahead with Apple Computer when their project was rejected by their respective employers, Atari and Hewlett-Packard. And when Thomas Watson was fired by National Cash Register in 1913, he joined up

---

Figure 2.1   The Entrepreneur's Quiz

Please circle only one correct answer below.

1. How were your parents employed?

   a. Both worked and were self-employed for most of their working lives.
   b. Both worked and were self-employed for part of their working lives.
   c. One parent was self-employed for most of his or her working life.
   d. One parent was self-employed at some point in his or her working life.
   e. Neither parent was ever self-employed.

2. Have you ever been fired from a job?

   a. more than once
   b. once
   c. never

3. Are you an immigrant, or were your parents or grandparents immigrants?

   a. I was born outside of the United States.
   b. At least one of my parents was born outside of the United States.
   c. At least one of my grandparents was born outside of the United States.
   d. My grandparents, my parents and I were all born in the United States.

4. Your work career has been primarily in:

   a. small business (under 100 employees)
   b. medium-sized business (100–500 employees)
   c. big business (over 500 employees)

5. Did you operate any businesses before you were 20?

   a. many
   b. a few
   c. none

6. What is your present age?

   a. 21–30
   b. 31–40
   c. 41–50
   d. 51 or over

7. You are the _____ child in the family.

   a. oldest
   b. middle
   c. youngest
   d. other

8. You are:

   a. married
   b. divorced
   c. single

9. Your highest level of formal education is:

   a. some high school
   b. high school diploma
   c. bachelor's degree
   d. master's degree
   e. doctoral degree

10. What is your primary motivation in starting a business?

    a. I want to make money.
    b. I don't like working for someone else.
    c. I want to be famous.
    d. I need an outlet for excess energy.

11. Your relationship to the parent who provided most of the family's income was:

    a. strained
    b. comfortable
    c. competitive
    d. nonexistent

12. You find the answers to difficult questions by:

    a. working hard
    b. working smart
    c. both

13. On whom do you rely for critical management advice?

    a. internal management teams
    b. external management professionals
    c. external financial professionals
    d. no one except myself

Figure 2.1   (continued)

---

14. If you were at the racetrack, which of these would you bet on?

    a. the daily double—a chance to make a killing
    b. a ten-to-one shot
    c. a three-to-one shot
    d. the two-to-one favorite

15. The only ingredient that is both necessary and sufficient for starting a business is:

    a. money
    b. customers
    c. an idea or product
    d. motivation and hard work

16. At a cocktail party you:

    a. are the life of the party
    b. never know what to say to people
    c. just fit into the crowd
    d. You never go to cocktail parties.

17. You tend to "fall in love" too quickly with:

    a. new product ideas
    b. new employees
    c. new manufacturing ideas
    d. new financial plans
    e. all of the above

18. Which of the following personality types is best suited to be your right-hand person?

    a. bright and energetic
    b. bright and lazy
    c. dumb and energetic

19. You accomplish tasks better because:

    a. you are always on time
    b. you are well organized
    c. you keep good records

20. You hate to discuss:

    a. problems involving employees
    b. expense accounts
    c. new management practices
    d. the future of the business

21. Given a choice, you would prefer:

    a. rolling dice with a one-in-three chance of winning
    b. working on a problem with a one-in-three chance of solving it in the time allocated

22. If you could choose between the following competitive professions, your choice would be:

    a. professional golf
    b. sales
    c. personnel counseling
    d. teaching

23. If you had to choose between working with a partner who is a close friend and working with a stranger who is an expert in your field, you would choose:

    a. the close friend
    b. the expert

24. In business situations that demand action, clarifying who is in charge will help produce results.

    a. Agree.
    b. Agree, with reservations.
    c. Disagree.

25. In playing a competitive game, you are concerned with:

    a. how well you play
    b. winning
    c. both of the above
    d. none of the above

Figure 2.1   (continued)

Score Key

1. a-10 b-5 c-5 d-2 e-0	8. a-10 b-2 c-2	14. a-0 b-2 c-10 d-3	20. a-8 b-10 c-0 d-0
2. a-10 b-7 c-0	9. a-2 b-3 c-8 d-10 e-4	15. a-0 b-10 c-0 d-0	21. a-0 b-15
3. a-5 b-4 c-3 d-0	10. a-0 b-15 c-0 d-0	16. a-5 b-10 c-3 d-5	22. a-3 b-10 c-0 d-0
4. a-10 b-7 c-0	11. a-10 b-5 c-10 d-5	17. a-5 b-5 c-5 d-5 e-15	23. a-0 b-10
5. a-10 b-7 c-0	12. a-0 b-0 c-10	18. a-2 b-10 c-0	24. a-10 b-2 c-0
6. a-8 b-10 c-5 d-2	13. a-0 b-10 c-0 d-5	19. a-5 b-15 c-5	25. a-8 b-15 c-10 d-0
7. a-15 b-2 c-0 d-0			

with the Computer-Tabulating-Recording Company and ran it until a month before his death in 1956. He also changed the company's name to IBM. Hugh Hefner, the founder of *Playboy* magazine, quit *Esquire* because management refused him a $5-a-week pay increase. The need to be right very often turns rejection into courage and courage into authority.

3. America is still the land of opportunity and a hotbed for entrepreneurship. The people who arrive on our shores (and at our airports) every day, be they Cuban, Korean or Vietnamese, can still turn hard work and enthusiasm into successful business enterprises. Many years ago, Korean born entrepreneur K. Philip Hwang worked his way through college by sweeping the floors of a Lake Tahoe casino. When Hwang took his company, Televideo, public, his personal stock holdings were valued at $750 million. Though it is far from a necessary ingredient for entrepreneurship, the need to succeed is often greater among those whose backgrounds contain an extra struggle to fit into society.

4. I've heard it said that "inside every corporate body, there's an entrepreneur struggling to escape. However, small business management is more than just a scaled-down version of big business management. The skills needed to run a big business are altogether different from those needed to orchestrate an entrepreneurial venture. *While the professional manager is skilled at protecting resources, the entrepreneurial manager is skilled at creating them.* Entrepreneurs are at their best when they can still control all aspects of the company. That's why so many successful entrepreneurs have been kicked out of the top spot when their companies outgrew their talents. Of course, that isn't always a tragedy. For many, it offers the opportunity (and the capital) to start all over again. They usually like that better (Steven Jobs, Ross Perot).

5. The enterprising adult first appears as the enterprising child. Coin and stamp collecting, mowing lawns, shoveling snow, promoting dances and rock concerts are all common examples of early business ventures. The paper route of today could be the Federal Express of tomorrow.

6. The average age of entrepreneurs has been steadily shifting downward since the late 1950s, when it was between 40 and 45 years. *Inc.* magazine listed 39 people under the age of 30 in its 1992 "500" private company ranking. My most recent research puts the highest concentration of entrepreneurs in their thirties, but people like Jobs and Wozniak of Apple Computer, Michael Dell of Dell Corporation, Ed DeCastro of Data General and Fred Smith of Federal Express all got their businesses off the ground while still in their twenties. About ten years ago, my good friend, Fran Jabara, a professor at Wichita State University in Kansas, started the Association of Collegiate Entrepreneurs (ACE). That's because college kids are doing it, too!

Some start even younger, like computer whiz Jonathan Rotenberg. Legend has it that the promoter of an upcoming public computer show solicited Rotenberg's advice. After conferring several times on the phone, the promoter suggested they meet for a drink to continue their discussions. "I can't," Rotenberg replied. "I'm only 15."

However, the emergence of the mid-career entrepreneur might cancel out this shift to younger entrepreneurs.

Whatever their age, entrepreneurs thrive on fighting the odds. Look at some of the crazy long shots that made it out of the garage and on to *Fortune* magazine's ranking of America's 100 fastest-growing companies. PictureTel (no. 14), the largest maker of videophones, was started by two 22-year-old MIT students soldering circuitboards in their apartment. Ma Bell had a big headstart on them. PictureTel founders, Jeffrey Bernstein and Brian Hinman, now 31, were mere toddlers when AT&T showed off a prototype Picturephone at the 1964 World's Fair. But the scrappy start-up made the breakthrough that is turning the vision into reality. Its videophones now lead in the high end of the market.

7. The answer to this question is usually the same. Entrepreneurs are most commonly the oldest children in a family. With an average of 2.5 children per American family, the chances of being the first child are less than 40 percent. However, entrepreneurs tend to be the oldest children more than 60 percent of the time.

In an interesting aside (and we're not quite sure what it means), a Mormon Church official has revealed that in cases of polygamous marriages, the first sons of the second or third marriage are generally more entrepreneurial than the first child of the first marriage.

8. Our research indicated that the vast majority of entrepreneurs are married. But then, most people in their thirties are married, so this alone is not a significant finding. However, follow-up studies show that most successful entrepreneurs have exceptionally supportive wives. (While our results did not provide conclusive results on female entrepreneurs, we suspect that their husbands would have to be equally supportive.) A supportive mate provides the love and stability necessary to balance the insecurity and stress of the job. A strained marriage, the pressures of a divorce or a turbulent love life will add too much pressure to an already strained business life.

It's also interesting to note that bankers and venture capitalists look a lot more favorably on entrepreneurs who are married than on those who are living with their mates without the benefit of clergy. This is more of a pragmatic attitude than a moralistic one. A venture capitalist remarked to me that, "If an entrepreneur isn't willing to make a commitment to the woman he loves, then I'll be damned if I'm going to make any financial commitment to him." It's the same controversial position once taken by former presidential candidate H. Ross Perot.

9. The question of formal education among entrepreneurs has always been controversial. Studies in the 1950s and 1960s showed that many entrepreneurs, like insurance great W. Clement Stone, hadn't finished high school. Polaroid's founder, Edwin Land, has long been held up as an example of an "entrepreneur in a hurry" because he dropped out of Harvard in his freshman year to get his business off the ground. Jobs and Wozniak of Apple were also college dropouts. The same goes for the richest man in America, Bill Gates of Microsoft.

However, our data indicate that the most common educational level achieved by entrepreneurs is the bachelor's degree, and the trend seems headed toward the MBA. Just the same, few entrepreneurs have the time or the patience to earn a doctorate. Notable exceptions include An Wang of Wang Laboratories, Robert Noyce and Gordon Moore of Intel and Robert Collings of Data Terminal Systems.

10. Entrepreneurs don't like working for anyone but themselves. While money is always a consideration, there are easier ways to make money than by going it alone. More often than not, money is a byproduct (albeit a welcome one) of an entrepreneur's motivation rather than the motivation itself.

11. These results really surprised me because past studies, including my own, have always emphasized the strained or competitive relationship between the entrepreneur and the income-producing parent (usually the father). The entrepreneur has traditionally been out to "pick up the pieces" for the family or to "show the old man," while at the same time seeking his grudging praise.

However, my latest study showed that a surprising percentage of the entrepreneurs we questioned had what they considered to be comfortable relationships with their income-producing parents. How do we explain this? To a large extent, we think it's directly related to the changing ages and educational backgrounds of the new entrepreneurs. The new entrepreneurs are not the children of the depression. Most have been afforded the luxury of a college education and have not had to drop out of high school to help support the family. Thus, the entrepreneur's innate independence has not come into such dramatic conflict with the father as it might have in the past. We still feel that a strained or competitive relationship best fits the entrepreneurial profile, though the nature of this relationship is no longer so black and white.

12. The difference between the hard worker and the smart worker is the difference between the hired hand and the boss. What's more, entrepreneurs usually enjoy what they're doing so much that they rarely notice how hard they're

really working. I've always believed that a decision is an action taken by an executive when the information he or she has gathered is so incomplete that the answer doesn't suggest itself. The entrepreneur's job is to make sure the answers always suggest themselves.

13. Entrepreneurs seldom rely on internal people for major policy decisions because employees often have pet projects to protect or personal axes to grind. What's more, internal managers seldom offer conflicting opinions on big decisions, so in the end the entrepreneur decides alone.

Outside financial sources are not good sounding boards for big decisions because they lack the imagination that characterizes most entrepreneurs. The most noble ambition of most bankers and accountants is to maintain the status quo.

When it comes to critical decisions, entrepreneurs most often rely on outside management consultants and other entrepreneurs. In fact, my follow-up work has shown that outside management professionals have played a role in every successful business I've studied, which wasn't the case when it came to unsuccessful ventures.

14. Contrary to popular belief, entrepreneurs are not high risk takers. They tend to set realistic and achievable goals, and when they do take risks, they're usually calculated risks. They are overly confident in their own skills and are much more willing to bet on their tennis or golf games than they are to buy lottery tickets or to bet on spectator sports. If an entrepreneur was in Atlantic City with just $10, chances are he or she would spend it on telephone calls and not in slot machines.

15. All businesses begin with orders, and orders can only come from customers. You might think you're in business when you've developed a prototype or raised capital, but bankers and venture capitalists only buy potential. It takes customers to buy products.

16. At a cocktail party you: Like billionaire Daniel Ludwig, many entrepreneurs will adamantly state that they have no hobbies. But that doesn't mean that they have no social life. In fact, entrepreneurs are very social people and, more often than not, very charming people. (Remember, entrepreneurs are people who get things done, and getting things done often involves charming the right banker or supplier.) And while they often talk only about things concerning themselves or their businesses, their enthusiasm is such that anything they talk about sounds interesting.

17. You tend to "fall in love" too quickly with: One of the biggest weaknesses that entrepreneurs face is their tendency to "fall in love" too easily. They go wild over new employees, products, suppliers, machines, methods and financial plans. Anything new excites them. But these affairs usually end

almost as suddenly as they begin. The problem is that during these affairs, entrepreneurs can alienate their staffs, become stubborn about listening to opposing views and lose their objectivity.

18. The natural inclination is to choose "bright and energetic" because that describes a personality like your own. But stop and think a minute. You're the boss. Would you be happy or efficient as someone else's assistant? Probably not. And you don't want to hire an entrepreneur to do a hired hand's job.

That's why the "bright and lazy" personality makes the best assistant. He's not out to prove himself, so he won't be butting heads with the entrepreneur at every turn. And while he's relieved at not having to make critical decisions, he's a whiz when it comes to implementing them. Why? Because, unlike the entrepreneur, he's good at delegating responsibilities. Getting other people to do the work for him is his specialty! As you get buffered you get better.

19. Organization is the fundamental principle on which all entrepreneurial ventures are based. Without it, no other principles matter. Organizational systems may differ, but you'll never find an entrepreneur who's without one. Some keep lists on their desks, crossing things off from the top and adding to the bottom. Others use notecards, keeping a file in their jacket pockets. And still others keep notes on scraps of paper, shuffling them from pocket to pocket in an elaborate filing and priority system. It doesn't matter how you do it, as long as it works. The small electronic vest-pocket computers are a current fad.

20. The only thing an entrepreneur likes less than discussing employee problems is discussing petty cash slips and expense accounts. Solving problems is what an entrepreneur does best, but personnel problems seldom require his intervention, so discussing them is just an irritating distraction. Expense accounts are even worse. An entrepreneur wants to know how much the salespeople are selling, not how much they're padding their expense accounts.

21. Entrepreneurs are participants, not observers; players, not fans. And to be an entrepreneur is to be an optimist, to believe that with the right amount of time and money, you can do anything.

Of course, chance plays a part in anyone's career—being in the right place at the right time; but entrepreneurs have a tendency to make their own chances. I'm reminded of the story about the shoe manufacturer who sent his two sons to the Mediterranean to scout out new markets. One wired back: "No point in staying on. No one here wears shoes." The other son wired back: "Terrific opportunities. Thousands still without shoes." Who do you think eventually took over the business?

22. Sales give instant feedback on your performance; it's the easiest job of all for measuring success. How does a personnel counselor or a teacher ever know if he's winning or losing? Entrepreneurs need immediate feedback and

are always capable of adjusting their strategies in order to win. *Some entrepreneurs brag that they play by the rules when they're winning and change the rules when they're losing so they can still win.* Although I don't endorse it (look what happened to John DeLorean), when it works it's known as the win-win strategy.

23. While friends are important, solving problems is clearly more important. Often, the best thing an entrepreneur can do for a friendship is to spare it the extra strain of a working relationship. By carefully dividing her work life and her social life, the entrepreneur ensures that business decisions will always be in the best interest of the business.

24. Everyone knows that a camel is a horse that was designed by a committee. Unless it's clear that one person is in charge, decisions are bound to suffer from a committee mentality.

25. Vince Lombardi is famous for saying, "Winning isn't everything, it's the only thing," but a lesser known quote of his is closer to the entrepreneur's philosophy. Looking back at a season, Lombardi was heard to remark, "We didn't lose any games last season, we just ran out of time twice."

Entrepreneuring is a competitive game, and an entrepreneur has to be prepared to run out of time, occasionally. Walt Disney, Henry Ford and Milton Hershey all experienced bankruptcy before experiencing success. The right answer to this question is *c* (both of the above), but the best answer is the game itself.

Your Entrepreneurial Profile

225–275	successful entrepreneur*
190–224	entrepreneur
175–189	latent entrepreneur
160–174	potential entrepreneur
150–159	borderline entrepreneur
Below 149	hired hand

■ The Shortcut to the Quiz

While the above traits characterize people who start businesses, I have been searching for three decades for one trait that was a single foolproof indicator. It had to be an accurate but quick litmus test.

---

*The CEM member profile is 234.

In 1986, at my 25-year Worcester Polytechnic Institute college (WPI) reunion, I hit upon it. It has not yet stood the test of time, but it looks good so far. Here's how to tell.

- *Entrepreneur.* Gets in the car and drives off. While driving, he or she adjusts the radio, air conditioner, lights, seats, mirror and seat belt. All of this is done at some peril as the car reaches maximum speed.

- *Hired hand.* Adjusts the radio, air conditioner, lights, seats, mirror and seat belt. Then starts the car and drives off.

- *Passenger.* To make the test infallible, the entrepreneur needs to be a passenger in a car operated by a hired hand. Some of them can't do it because it involves giving up too much control. But here's what happens when they are passengers.

    As the driver adjusts the radio, mirror, air conditioning, seat, seat belt and vents, the entrepreneur-passenger shouts out uncontrollably: "For God's sake, start the car!"

So far, it looks like my Rosetta stone.

■ The Synergy of the Entrepreneur

After fighting a five-day battle, an American soldier walked nearly 75 miles through the French countryside to a small village of about 50 homes. He was so tired and hungry he could hardly raise his hand to knock on the door. An angry woman opened the door and demanded to know the nature of his business. He asked for a piece of bread, a glass of water or anything she could spare. She screamed at him to go away, saying she could hardly feed herself as she angrily slammed the door in his face.

The soldier then walked to a second house and asked for food or water. The owner refused even more angrily than the woman in the first house.

So the soldier walked a bit farther until his gaze fell on a cracked but nevertheless functioning water fountain in the middle of the town square.

The soldier drank as much water as his stomach could hold and, in the middle of the park, started a small fire. He filled his helmet with water, placed two average-sized stones in it and began stirring the mixture over the fire.

A little boy approached and asked what he was doing. The soldier replied, "I am making the most delicious stone soup in the whole world." The boy asked if he could have some. "Certainly," the soldier replied, "but the soup needs a few vegetables to make it really delicious." The boy said his parents had a few carrots at home and ran to get them. Meanwhile, a married couple came along and asked the soldier what he was doing. "I'm making the most delicious stone soup in the whole world." They asked if he would share his bounty with them, and he replied, "Of course, but I need a soup bone and perhaps some spices to make this soup the very best." The wife rushed home to find something to contribute to the mixture. While she was gone, an old woman passed through and helped the mixture by adding a few potatoes. Within an hour, several more people had contributed to the soup.

At just the right moment, the starving soldier removed the stones and ladled out a cup of marvelous stone soup to each person who had contributed ingredients. There still was plenty left over for him to enjoy.

In this children's story, the soldier is a catalyst who brings these individuals together for their mutual gain. None of those who enjoyed the delicious soup had the ingredients to make it individually. The soldier's ingenuity brought everyone together for the common good. This illustrates synergy and entrepreneurship at its best.

■ ■

3

Starting Your Own Business

This is a difficult chapter to write because you really can't tell someone how to start a business, just as you can't pick someone's spouse. It's too personal a matter. If you ever fixed up two friends for a date and thought they would hit it off only to discover there was no chemistry, you know what I mean. With that in mind, I won't try to tell you what business to start, but I will suggest reliable sources of information so you can decide for yourself. However, I suggest the business you start should be in a growth industry. That way, marginal performance can still yield positive results.

■ How To Spot a Growth Industry

Remember the Academy Award winning movie *The Graduate,* starring Dustin Hoffman? It began with a cocktail party scene that is still considered a classic. While standing by the swimming pool at his graduation party, Dustin Hoffman is approached by one of his parents' friends, a successful businessman, who whispers in his ear a single word he thinks is the key to the young man's future: "Plastics." It was his way of suggesting to the new graduate it is easier to be successful if you begin your career in a growth industry.

Entrepreneurs are cutting-edge thinkers. Because they are able to spot trends, they are part of the early group in any success. They make the success happen not by watching, but by participating.

Let me share a technique entrepreneurs use to spot growth industries. It's a process, not a single solution, and it involves watching the evolution of new publications.

Have you noticed that there are too many magazines on the newsstands? And they change faster than airline schedules. That's because there is a host of magazine entrepreneurs who are watching trends, and as soon as a new niche appears, they flood it with magazines. Then, over time, the good ones survive and Darwin's principles of natural selection prevail. Consequently, countless magazines fold every year.

To spot a growth industry, I suggest watching the titles of new magazines. They can tell you when robotics or solar energy or biotechnology or whatever is hot. When a new magazine appears, it acts as a catalyst to spread and unite a trend. As a shared informational medium, it pulls together the diverse aspects of a movement so it can get the full power of a hurricane behind it. A good way to keep track of new magazines is by subscribing to *Folio,* the magazine of magazine management (P.O. Box 4949, Stanford, CT 06907-0949, 203/358-9900).

■ How To Get an Eight-Year Lead Time

Studying magazine titles gives you a four-year lead time on most people. Entrepreneurs like an advantage, but four years is not enough. You can double that to an eight-year lead time by watching what the magazine entrepreneurs watch. How and when do they get the idea to launch a new magazine? What indicators do they watch?

To get the answers, I asked the founder of *Inc.* magazine, Bernie Goldhirsch. Before launching *Inc.,* he launched another magazine called *Sail.* After that, he failed with a handful of technology-based magazines, despite the fact that he is an MIT-trained electrical engineer. Nonetheless, Bernie's words of wisdom are worth repeating. He says he watches the newsletter industry.

When an industry has a few newsletters succeeding, it becomes a candidate for a magazine. Before there was a recognized robotics industry, genetics industry or women's movement, there were newsletters in those fields. The magazines follow the newsletters.

Bernie watches the flow of new newsletters from two sources:

■ The *Newsletter on Newsletters,* published by the Newsletter Clearinghouse, P.O. Box 311, Rhinebeck, NY 12572, 914/876-2081

■ Newsletter Publishers Association, 1401 Wilson Blvd., Arlington, VA 22209, 703/527-2333

Newsletter directories can also help you gauge what fields are underserved or overcrowded. Two of the most comprehensive directories are *The Oxbridge Directory of Newsletters* and Gale's *Newsletters in Print.* The latter is a descriptive guide to more than 11,000 subscription, membership and free newsletters, bulletins, digests, updates and similar serial publications issued in the United States and Canada.

■ Checklists for Starting a Small Business

Before entering a new business venture, use a checklist to guide you in analyzing all the elements necessary for success. The checklist exposes variables that might be forgotten in the rush to start a business. It's also wise to look over a checklist after you begin a business venture. The following nine checklists (Figures 3.1–3.9) ask you to award yourself points in key areas ranging from financing to employee relations. Give yourself the highest possible number of points on each scale if you have an exceptionally strong plus in the area. Give yourself the lowest number of points (zero) if you are weak in an area.

Figure 3.1   Are You Equipped for a Business Venture?

		Points
1.	Have you ever been in business for yourself before?	0–5
2.	Have you succeeded in business for yourself before?	0–10
3.	Have you ever previously rated your abilities for managing a growing business enterprise?	0–3
4.	Have you taken any courses or special training that will help you in your own business?	0–5
5.	Have you read any books about starting your own business?	0–3
6.	Have you talked to friends who have started their own businesses?	0–3
7.	Have you checked the Entrepreneur's Quiz or any of the other entrepreneurial assessment tools offered by the Center for Entrepreneurial Management?	0–5
8.	Has anyone in your family—your father, mother, brother or sister—been self-employed? Have you spoken to them about your venture?	0–7

Background
Sum

Average score: 31 out of a possible 41 points

Figure 3.2 How Good Is Your Idea?

	Points
1. Is your idea an original idea? Does it have significant merit or is it a new package for an old idea?	0–7
2. Is it your idea? Will you be able to generate extensions of this idea?	0–3
3. How difficult would it be for someone else to have the idea?	0–5
4. Have you checked to see if someone else has already had the same idea? Is your idea patentable? Have you checked the patent office?	0–10
5. Have you checked to see if other companies exist that produce the same product?	0–4
6. Have you checked *Thomas Register* to see if this product or service is offered?	0–5
7. Have you discussed or disclosed your idea to an expert in the area?	0–3
8. Have you talked to inventors about your idea?	0–3
9. Have you analyzed the recent sales trends in this business?	0–5
10. Do you know the volume and profitability of competitors?	0–5
11. Is there a single large successful competitor who is highly profitable?	0–10
12. Have you attempted to obtain sales orders, commitments or letters of intent from potential customers?	0–15
13. Do other services or products like yours exist?	0–5
	Idea Sum

Average score: 65 out of a possible 75 points

Figure 3.3   How about Money?

	Points
1. Have you saved enough money to start the business on your own?	0–15
2. Do you know how much money you'll need to get the business started?	0–10
3. How much of your money can you put into the business versus how much money is needed? Do you need a partner to supply money?	0–15
4. Do you know what sales volume is necessary to break even?	0–7
5. Will it take less than three years before your business reaches the breakeven sales volume?	0–10
6. Do you know how much credit your suppliers will provide? Do you know the terms of payment in your industry?	0–5
7. What are the normal terms for selling in your industry?	0–3
8. Are you aware of sources that will help finance your business in the event that you exhaust your initial capital?	0–4
9. Have you talked to a banker about your plans for a new business?	0–3
10. Have you talked to a lawyer about your plans for a new business?	0–3
11. Have you talked to an accountant about your plans for a new business?	0–3
12. Have you found a good location for your business?	0–10
13. Does the location provide expansion possibilities?	0–5
14. Will the location require extensive leasehold improvement expenditures?	0–5
15. Have you examined the trade-off of buying instead of leasing a facility?	0–5
16. Is the location convenient for parking and public transportation? Is it accessible to employees, suppliers and customers?	0–5
17. Have you checked the lease and zoning requirements?	0–3
18. Did you evaluate several locations before making your final selection?	0–3
19. Have you made a scaled layout of your office or work area to study work flow or customer flow?	0–7
20. Are you a good manager of money?	0–15
	Money Sum

Average score: 111 out of a possible 136 points

Figure 3.4 Have You Investigated the Potential Success of Your Business?

	Points
1. Have you compared the standard operating ratios for your business with industry averages and with Dun & Bradstreet?	0–2
2. Have you decided firmly on a single legal form of organization? Have you researched all the alternatives?	0–5
3. Have you written down a statement of what you want to do to help your customers, suppliers and employees understand the purpose of your business?	0–15
4. Have you answered the difficult question, What business am I in?	0–15
	Success Sum

Average score: 25 out of a possible 37 points

Figure 3.5 Risk Management

	Points
1. Have you considered the impact on your business of government regulatory agencies like OSHA, Equal Employment Opportunity Commission, etc.?	0–3
2. Have you made allowances for unpredictable expenses resulting from uninsured risks such as bad debts, shoplifting or fire?	0–5
3. Do you know the kind of insurance that you should purchase? Should you purchase product liability insurance?	0–4
4. Have you determined which hazards you should insure against?	0–5
	Risk Sum

Average score: 15 out of a possible 17 points

Figure 3.6 Employee Relations and Purchasing

	Points
1. Have you hired your first employee? Does he or she have the requisite skills to grow on the job as well as do the job in the initial phases?	0–10
2. Have you prepared a general wage structure and does it compare favorably with prevailing wage rates?	0–7
3. Are your working conditions desirable?	0–10
4. If you plan to employ your friends and relatives, are you sure the family will not get in the way of the business?	0–10
5. Are you planning an employee incentive program?	0–3
6. If so, is it your program or their program?	0–7
7. Have you evaluated alternative sources of supply?	0–7
8. Have you carefully analyzed the pros and cons of each source of supply? Each vendor? Have you avoided friendships with salespeople or vendors so that your buying decisions will not be influenced by personal feelings?	0–5
9. Have you investigated other sources of supply that are not available locally but may be accessed through direct mail? Cooperative purchasing? overseas pricing?	0–5
	People Sum

Average score: 43 out of a possible 64 points

Figure 3.7   Advertising and Sales Promotion

		Points
1.	Do you have copies of your competitors' advertisements for the last 12 months?	0–5
2.	Do you know how much your competitors are spending on each advertisement and their percentage of sales?	0–5
3.	Have you defined your customer? Do you know how and why your customer buys?	0–15
4.	Have you determined the media or the messages that will influence your customers' buying habits?	0–7
5.	Do you know what successful and unsuccessful advertising will be for your business?	0–7
6.	Have you investigated direct mailing as an alternative?	0–5
7.	Do you have a good mailing list?	0–5
8.	Have you selected the most promising features and benefits of your business to promote?	0–10
9.	Do you know which media or methods are most suitable for advertising your business?	0–12
10.	Do you know the cost of these media?	0–5
11.	Have you discussed marketing issues that are central to your business with a marketing expert?	0–15

Advertising
Sum

Average score: 65 out of a possible 89 points

Figure 3.8 Pricing

	Points
1. Have you decided to price your product on the basis of its cost or on what the competitors charge for their product? Shouldn't you price it based upon what the market will bear?	0–15
2. Have you thought through the advantages of being a price leader or a price follower?	0–10
3. Have you considered your competitors' reactions to any of your pricing policies?	0–7
4. Have you considered the relative importance of each market segment with different pricing policies?	0–5
5. Have you investigated pricing issues to be sure you're not in violation of any of the codes? (Robinson-Patman, etc.)	0–3
6. Is your pricing sufficient so that you will make a profit on each of the products you sell?	0–5
7. Do you know what your contribution margin is on each product?	0–4
8. Has it taken into account your breakeven volume?	0–5
9. Do you anticipate having to raise or lower your price to meet competitors in the future?	0–5
10. Do you offer special discounts for special customers? Is this a generally known policy?	0–3
11. Have you developed a chart of accounts to classify your expenses?	0–3
12. Do you know what your largest expense items are? Can you control or reduce these expenses?	0–5
13. Have you attempted to control these expenses from the very beginning?	0–5
14. Do you have a flexible expense budget to be able to handle unexpected expenses?	0–7
	Pricing Sum

Average score: 55 out of a possible 89 points

Figure 3.9 Miscellaneous

	Points
1. Have you complied with the local town government regulations by filing the appropriate forms?	0–2
2. Have you done the same for the state and the federal government?	0–2
3. Have you set up an adequate recordkeeping system to generate your tax payments and especially your payroll taxes?	0–3
4. Is your chart of accounts sensible? Are there items that are too large or too small?	0–2
5. Will you be able to compare your performance with existing standard operating ratios? (D&B)	0–2
6. Have you obtained a Social Security number or tax identification number for your business?	0–2
7. Is your business clear from sales tax exemptions?	0–2
8. Have you provided for a sense of security about these government issues to all your employees?	0–2
9. Have you complied with regulations about copyrighting, trademarks, brand names and trade names?	0–3
10. Have you figured out whether or not you could make more money working for someone else?	0–5
11. Are you prepared to invest boundless energy and time in this business venture?	0–8
12. Does your family go along with your desire to start a business?	0–15
13. Do you know how to discover the second product or second location or second feature of your business?	0–8
14. Have you spoken to the Small Business Administration for help?	0–10
15. Have you secured any of its pamphlets?	0–3
16. Have you gotten help from any other source, such as Score, Ace or the Small Business Institute?	0–5
	Misc. Sum

Average score: 57 out of a possible 74 points

Following in Figure 3.10 is a breakdown of scores for each checklist.

Figure 3.10 Checklist Scoring

	Average Score	Total Possible Score
1. Are you equipped for a business venture—8 questions	31	41
2. How good is your idea—3 questions	65	75
3. How about money—20 questions	111	136
4. Have you investigated the potential success of your business—4 questions	25	37
5. Risk management—4 questions	15	17
6. Employee relations and purchasing—9 questions	43	64
7. Advertising and sales promotion—11 questions	65	89
8. Pricing—14 questions	55	89
9. Miscellaneous—16 questions	57	74
Total	467	622
Your Sum		
Success Sum		
Pricing Sum		

■ Analyzing Your Start-Up Costs

If you completed all the checklists in this chapter, you've already done some hard work and serious thinking. That's a start, but before moving on to specific issues such as buying, franchising and negotiating, which I'll cover in later chapters, you must have some idea of what your enterprise will cost. Maybe you're thinking too big—or too small. The worksheets in Figures 3.11 and 3.12 will help you get a grip on start-up expenses so that you can define the scope of your business.

Figure 3.11 Estimated Start-Up Costs

ESTIMATED MONTHLY EXPENSES		
ITEM	Your estimate of monthly expenses based on sales of $_____ per year **Column 1**	Your estimate of how much cash you need to start your business (See col. 3) **Column 2**	What to put in column 2 (These figures are typical for one kind of business. You will have to decide how many months to allow for in your business.) **Column 3**
Salary of owner-manager	$	$	2 times column 1
All other salaries and wages			3 times column 1
Rent			3 times column 1
Advertising			3 times column 1
Delivery expenses			3 times column 1
Supplies			3 times column 1
Telephone and telegraph			3 times column 1
Other utilities			3 times column 1
Insurance			Payment required by insurance company
Taxes, including Social Security			4 times column 1
Interest			3 times column 1
Maintenance			3 times column 1

Figure 3.11 (continued)

Legal and other professional fees		3 times column 1
Miscellaneous		3 times column 1
STARTING COSTS YOU ONLY HAVE TO PAY ONCE		Leave column 2 blank
Fixtures and equipment		Fill in worksheet on page 49 and put the total here
Decorating and remodeling		Talk it over with a contractor
Installation of fixtures and equipment		Talk to suppliers from whom you buy these
Starting inventory		Suppliers will probably help you estimate this
Deposits with public utilities		Find out from utilities companies
Legal and other professional fees		Lawyer, accountant and so on
Licenses and permits		Find out from city offices what you have to have
Advertising and promotion for opening		Estimate what you'll use
Accounts receivable		What you need to buy more stock until credit customers pay
Cash		For unexpected expenses or losses, special purchases, etc.
Other		Make a separate list and enter total
TOTAL ESTIMATED CASH YOU NEED TO START WITH	$	Add up all the numbers in column 2

Figure 3.12 List of Furniture, Fixtures and Equipment

Leave out or add items to suit your business. Use separate sheets to list exactly what you need for each of the items below.	If you plan to pay cash in full, enter the full amount below and in the last column.	If you are going to pay by installments, fill out the columns below. Enter in the last column your downpayment plus at least one installment.			Estimate of the cash you need for furniture, fixtures and equipment
		Price	Down-payment	Amount of each installment	
Counters	$	$	$	$	$
Storage shelves, cabinets					
Display stands, shelves, tables					
Cash register					
Safe					
Window display fixtures					
Special lighting					
Delivery equipment if needed					
TOTAL FURNITURE, FIXTURES, AND EQUIPMENT (Enter this figure also in worksheet 2 under "Starting Costs You Only Have To Pay Once," page 20.)					$

■ Start-Up Resources

In running a business, you want to do all you can for yourself, but it's equally important to know where to find information or training when you need it. Check out what's available in libraries and bookstores in your area. Contact the chamber of commerce, government agencies, local business groups and professional associations in your field. Find out about seminars or adult education classes offered through local universities.

A good book on starting a business has the unlikely title *How to Get Rich* (Contemporary Books, 1991). Author Chuck Whitlock shows 35 examples of businesses you can start by using market niching techniques. My own book, *How to Start, Finance and Manage Your Own Small Business* (Simon & Schuster, 1988), is considered a classic in this field and has helped thousands launch their businesses. Most bookstores are happy to order these or any other available title that is not on their shelves.

The U.S. Small Business Administration has myriad pamphlets, books, videotapes and other resources for would-be entrepreneurs. They can be reached toll-free in Washington, D.C. at 800/827-5722 or at any of the regional offices around the country.

You can even get help from outplacement services. One of the best in the country is Enterchange Southwest, Inc. in Dallas (214/702-9484).

Running a business takes guts. You've got to decide what you need and then go after it. *Good luck.*

4

Franchising

Fred DeLuca needed cash. At 17, he was ready for college and unless he raised some money fast, he knew he couldn't cover his first-year expenses at Connecticut's University of Bridgeport. As it turned out, DeLuca's solution for financing his college education led to one of the biggest franchising success stories of the late '80s and early '90s. But, just then, back in 1965, all he wanted was a financial fix.

DeLuca approached a wealthy family friend for the money. He recalls hoping that Peter Buck, a nuclear physicist, would reach into his pocket and pull out a big stack of $10 bills. Instead, Buck offered something more valuable—a business proposition. Instead of a gift or loan, he gave the youngster $1,000 to open a submarine sandwich shop. And, so, Pete's Submarines of Bridgeport was born.

After a slow start (and a name change), the partners added 15 more sandwich shops in the following eight years. The chain had potential for further growth, but the traditional method of building and operating company-owned stores was proving to be slow and costly. The choice of an alternative wasn't hard to make. McDonald's and Kentucky Fried Chicken, among others, had set an excellent example by franchising, and it was in that direction that DeLuca turned to expand his business.

More than 25 years after it was started as a collegiate money-making venture, this submarine sandwich idea has become the pacesetter among sandwich chains, setting a growth standard believed to be untouched by even mega-outlet food giants such as McDonald's or Domino's Pizza. In a single year,

1988, Subway, as the franchise is now called, opened more than 1,000 outlets, a feat never previously accomplished by a single chain.

Of course, opening a sandwich shop isn't a rocket scientist type of proposition. All one needs is money (even someone else's money) and desire. Even making that shop a success isn't a superhuman task. Combine hard work, a good product and a reasonably decent location, and you can be the local roast beef and salami king. But to establish and successfully duplicate such a store a few thousand times across the country and around the world takes more than a profitable outlet (or even a few such outlets). It takes one of two things: nearly unlimited capital (literally billions of dollars) or the proven, synergistic power of franchising.

So, if you happen to have a couple of billion dollars lying around in a family trust, or a friendly banker whose loan checks come preprinted with nine zeros, then what follows will likely not be of much interest to you. But if you have a desire to become part of—or simply learn more about—franchising, the successful and growing form of business the U.S. Department of Commerce has called "the wave of the future," this book is the source you've been looking for.

■ What Is Franchising?

Franchising is a broad term that describes a relationship between two or more parties. In general, the purpose of this relationship is to distribute goods or services. The two primary types of franchise systems in the United States are Product or trade name franchising and business-format franchising.

Product or trade name franchising is franchising in its most limited form. It consists of a manufacturer granting another party a license to sell goods produced by the manufacturer. Principal examples of this form of franchising include sales of cars through dealerships, gasoline through service stations and soft drinks through local bottlers.

The other type of franchising, which is called business format franchising, is what most people call franchising. It means expanding your business the way Holiday Inn, McDonald's and Kentucky Fried Chicken do.

■ Do You Have What It Takes To Become a Franchisee?

Being a franchisee isn't for everyone. It isn't the same as owning a nonfranchised business, neither is it the same as working for someone else. Being a franchisee is a unique hybrid of both boss and employee—you own and run your franchised outlet, but you follow the system and dictates of the franchisor who has (presumably) perfected the business. In return for the franchisor's expertise, support and established reputation, you pay a percentage of your sales. In the best cases, this is a classic synergistic win-win situation. However, it takes a certain type of personality with specific working traits and temperaments to maintain the delicate balance of a franchisee.

Don Boroian, CEO of Francorp, a franchise consulting firm in Chicago, used to say that in the early days of franchising, before regulation weeded out the dubious franchisors, there were two important tests for potential franchisees; the *check test* and the *mirror test*. First, did the franchisee's check clear the bank? And second, if you held a mirror under his nose, did it fog up, meaning the candidate was still breathing? Furthermore, Don joked, some franchisors didn't believe the mirror test was that important, just as long as the check cleared!

This story exemplifies how much times have changed. Even if franchisee screening wasn't that loose and cynical back then, it sure has come a long way since.

Today, franchisors realize that a franchise that fails due to the choice of an unqualified franchisee costs them far more in time, money and reputation than the quick infusion of up-front money is ever worth. They know what they want when it comes to franchisees, and to determine who does (or doesn't) have these traits, a growing number of franchisors have turned to some form of testing. How do you measure up against the general traits they are looking for?

To help answer this question, I have gathered some solid data. Don's company, Francorp, in association with DePaul University in Chicago, has conducted extensive surveys of franchisors regarding the marketing and sales of franchises. A special section of the most recent edition of this poll asked respondents to choose, from a list of two dozen, the traits they found most important among their most successful franchisees. A total of 265 franchisors representing more than 40,000 franchised units responded to the survey. With the assistance of Dr. Harry E. "Bud" Gunn, a clinical psychologist noted for his job-related diagnostic tests, I used these responses to create the following test for prospective franchisees. This test has been used in practice by Francorp and has appeared in similar form in the book, *How to Buy and Manage a Franchise,* by Mancuso and Boroian (Simon & Schuster, 1993).

The test in Figure 4.1 is designed to measure your aptitude to be a franchisee, not your worth as a person or your overall general business acumen. As I have noted, the life of a franchisee is not for everyone—and it is important to find out if it is right for you before investing your time and money. In order to determine your potential for success as a franchisee, answer the questions in terms of your own feelings and experiences, rather than what you think a successful franchisee would say.

Figure 4.1   Franchisee Aptitude Test

For questions 1–16, circle the answer that *best* describes you or that you most agree with:

1. I have generally been regarded as:

    a. one who loves to plan vacations
    b. always being willing to work hard
    c. one who seeks benefits and rewards for my work
    d. being easy to supervise

2. Financially, I:

    a. am very conservative
    b. am very liberal
    c. have always been able to put money aside
    d. have never been well off

3. Taking directions from others is:

    a. one of my strong talents
    b. something I do not like
    c. often a must
    d. acceptable if not constantly required

4. Work-related pressure:

    a. can cause physical illness
    b. is something I try to avoid
    c. is a definite problem in business today
    d. seldom causes me any discomfort

5. I have generally been regarded as having:

    a. the ability to sell things
    b. a good grasp of what makes people tick
    c. physical strength
    d. emotional warmth

6. To reach one's optimum level of success, one must:

    a. have luck on her side
    b. be happy in his work
    c. be willing to take risks
    d. know the right people

7. Personally, I:

   a. am dissatisfied with my current profession
   b. have had a variety of life experiences
   c. have strong business and sales skills
   d. have not had much business experience

8. A major factor in business success is:

   a. an appetite to learn more about what you do
   b. a happy and stable personal life
   c. physical stamina
   d. extensive business experience

9. I am *best* described as:

   a. an intelligent person
   b. a highly verbal person
   c. a hard-driving person
   d. a person who can relate to other people

10. A strong desire to learn is:

    a. a valuable asset, both personally and professionally
    b. often necessary to advance in business
    c. not very important once you complete school
    d. uncommon in the business world

11. When a superior tells me what to do, I:

    a. wish I had his job so I could give orders
    b. often try to present a new, more efficient way of doing the task
    c. secretly resent being ordered around
    d. learn from the instructions and complete the task

12. To succeed in business, it is often more important to be hard working than to be a creative, talented person:

    a. strongly agree
    b. agree
    c. disagree
    d. strongly disagree

13. I have been best known for:

    a. getting involved in my community
    b. having good general business knowledge and skills
    c. being a good parent
    d. my work experience with a large company organization

Figure 4.1   (continued)

---

14. As a business owner, it would be most important to me to:

    a. provide jobs for my family
    b. be well thought of by my staff
    c. be able to set my own work schedule
    d. be closely aware of and prudent with my finances

15. Work hours should be:

    a. as long as needed
    b. paid for, especially for the boss
    c. flexible—long only when needed for special projects
    d. equally divided among all employees

16. A description of someone with a good chance to succeed in business is someone who:

    a. likes to get away regularly to avoid stress
    b. is always curious to learn more about doing his job
    c. works best by himself
    d. has a business degree from a top university

    For questions 17–30, pick the statement that *best* describes you.

17. a. I have a strong affinity for sales.

    b. I am highly energetic.

18. a. I have moderate experience in the type of business I would like to get into.

    b. I take direction well.

19. a. I am a creative person.

    b. I am a good listener.

20. a. I am a previous business owner.

    b. I am able to fully commit my finances to my business.

21. a. I don't mind working long hours.

    b. I have strong corporate skills.

22. a. I am a very careful, organized person.

    b. I am a people-oriented person.

23. a. I am a charitable person.

    b. I am a diplomatic person.

24. a. I am highly spontaneous.

    b. I am highly goal-directed.

25. a. I am able to take charge with people.

    b. I am a quick decision maker.

26. a. I have some basic financial knowledge.

    b. I have previous management experience.

27. a. I need to be in control.

    b. I can take directions from others.

28. a. I have extensive business skills.

    b. I am always willing to do what it takes to get things done.

29. a. I often use weekends to unwind.

    b. I am very resistant to stress.

30. a. I have money in the bank.

    b. I am willing to do without if necessary.

31. For this question, circle the five statements that are *least* like you.

    a. I am a slow starter.
    b. I can sell anything.
    c. I prefer to work by myself.
    d. I am interested in learning new skills.
    e. I would rather live spontaneously than set long-range goals.
    f. I thrive on stressful, busy, deadline situations.
    g. I work best by taking charge and issuing orders.
    h. I am rich in people skills.
    i. I prefer large corporate environments.
    j. I have a history of working long hours at favored activities.

■ Scoring

For each answer you chose, give yourself the corresponding amount of points listed below:

1. a—0,	b—4,	c—0,	d—2	17. a—2,	b—1	
2. a—2,	b—0,	c—4,	d—0	18. a—1,	b—2	
3. a—4,	b—0,	c—2,	d—1	19. a—1,	b—2	
4. a—0,	b—0,	c—1,	d—4	20. a—1,	b—2	
5. a—4,	b—2,	c—0,	d—0	21. a—2,	b—1	
6. a—0,	b—2,	c—4,	d—0	22. a—1,	b—2	
7. a—0,	b—2,	c—4,	d—0	23. a—1,	b—2	
8. a—4,	b—1,	c—0,	d—3	24. a—1,	b—2	
9. a—1,	b—0,	c—2,	d—4	25. a—2,	b—1	
10. a—4,	b—2,	c—0,	d—0	26. a—2,	b—1	
11. a—0,	b—2,	c—0,	d—4	27. a—1,	b—2	
12. a—4,	b—3,	c—0,	d—0	28. a—1,	b—2	
13. a—0,	b—4,	c—2,	d—1	29. a—1,	b—2	
14. a—1,	b—0,	c—0,	d—4	30. a—2,	b—1	
15. a—4,	b—0,	c—2,	d—0	31. a—1,	b—0,	c—1, d—0,
16. a—0,	b—4,	c—1,	d—1	e—1,	f—0,	g—1, h—0,
				i—1,	j—0	

Total points possible: 97

Ratings

97–79 Points: A Prime Candidate.   Congratulations! If you have answered the quiz questions frankly and received a score in this range, your personality traits, attitude, experience and temperament are good matches with the attributes many franchisors say are found in their most successful franchisees. You likely have a well-defined desire to learn and a willingness to follow directions in the quest for your own success. If you are financially able to do so, I strongly suggest that you pursue becoming a franchisee.

79–50 Points: A Potential Candidate.   Many of your traits are close to those found in top franchisee candidates; however, you may not be completely committed to the concept of running a franchised outlet of someone else's business. Although you may be interested in becoming a franchisee, your quiz answers differ from those of more "traditional" candidates; perhaps you have a strong streak of independence or are more comfortable giving directions than taking them. If you can ascertain where you differ from the "model" franchisee—by reading the following section analyzing important traits—you may be able to determine if these are fundamental differences or merely slight discrepancies. If the latter is true, you might be a good franchisee candidate.

50–0 Points: A Questionable Candidate.   A low score on this test might indicate that you would be more comfortable and successful as an independent business owner or a salaried employee. You may be more independent and have a stronger business background than most franchisees. Rather than trying to squeeze your individual talents into a field for which you may not be suited, you should probably seek other opportunities. If you still feel strongly committed to becoming a franchisee, examine how your test responses differ from the suggested answers. This can uncover areas in your personality or background that you need to reassess to improve your chances of becoming a successful franchisee. I will examine those traits and show you which ones *are* and *aren't* judged to be important to success as a franchisee.

■ Traits of Successful Franchisees

Nearly 90 percent of the respondents to the Francorp/DePaul survey reported having rejected financially qualified applicants because they lacked other qualifications that were judged to be more important to the long-term well-being of the franchise. What does it take to make a successful franchisee? How do your own skills, desires and experiences compare to those found among a sampling of the most successful franchisees extant? For example, how important is it to have previous experience in the franchisor's field, or to have worked for a large corporation? What are the most common traits that franchisors are looking for in prospective franchisees?

The Most Important Traits

Most of the respondents judged the following characteristics to be critical to a franchisee's success:

Eagerness To Learn.   More than three-quarters of the survey's respondents chose this trait as critical. This comes as little surprise because franchising can be boiled down to two tasks: teaching and systematization. Franchisors teach their franchisees how to run the business (in the case of conversion franchises, franchisees learn a modified—and, presumably, an improved—way of doing business); they must then repeat their lessons over and over as they serve their customers. Therefore, it follows that an eagerness to learn would serve a franchisee well. This trait is not to be confused with having an education. Although it is a definite advantage to have a high school education—and some college can be helpful—less than 10 percent of the franchisors in the survey said that any particular level of formal education was a critical requirement.

Willingness To Work Long Hours.   The fact that more than two-thirds of all respondents identified this as a critical trait clearly underscores the point there is no easy road to success in business ownership. Simply put, franchisees who want to succeed can expect to work long and hard hours to make their businesses successful, especially in the early days. You will have little or no staff to rely upon except, perhaps, unpaid family members—quite a different situation from the backgrounds of most corporate executives. Franchisors require this sort of devotion from their franchisees, and those who are aware of this expectation have a better chance of making it than those who may be less committed to taking on a large workload. It's definitely a case of perspiration, not inspiration.

Highly Developed People Skills.   Franchisees have to artfully and diplomatically deal with suppliers, employees, franchisor personnel and, most importantly, their customers. To do so, franchisees need to be able to express themselves, to listen and to have patience in dealing with a variety of situations. Accordingly, franchisors look for individuals who are at least somewhat outgoing, communicative and able to instill confidence in those around them. We can't stress enough the need to be a good listener. The good news is that this skill can be taught. Remember—God gave us two ears and only one mouth.

Sales Ability.   Whether it's pizzas, pets or paint jobs, every franchise sells something. And while you need not be a master salesperson to survive or succeed as a franchisee, you will need at least some level of sales ability. In a way, the evaluation of this ability starts the instant you meet with a franchisor—in the way you present yourself, the way you enumerate your skills and the way you handle questions. In other words, the franchisor will evaluate how you "sell" yourself. Again, this is a skill that can be learned. Just notice how many sales seminars are conducted every year.

Resistance To Stress. It's your 12th straight hour working at your franchised outlet. The phone is ringing, a customer's baby is crying, an employee needs you to handle a dispute with an irate customer, and you're behind in getting your required paperwork filled out and sent to the franchisor's headquarters. A bad day? Sure, but it could be *any* day in the life of a new franchisee. Can your temperament handle these stressful situations? Can you focus on necessary tasks, no matter what distractions or deadlines accompany them? Franchisors know that being a franchisee is often stressful, so they will want to know how well you handle pressure. (This is another skill that can be learned—and probably should be by most businesspeople!)

Ability To Take Directions. Similar to "eagerness to learn" (yet with a subtle difference), this trait was rated as critical by more than half of the franchisors who responded to the survey. Franchisees must trust in the methods the franchisor has developed; directions and requirements are not made capriciously, but rather to benefit the franchisee and the rest of the franchise system. Consequently, franchisees must be able to subordinate their opinions to those of the franchisor. An unyielding, "my way or the highway" type of person who chafes at taking suggestions or orders is not a good candidate to become a successful franchisee.

Having Money in Reserve. More than 90 percent of respondents rated this trait as critical or at least somewhat important to the success of a franchisee. This may contradict the common perception of a franchisee who has his or her last dime invested in the venture, but it just makes good business sense. Yes, franchisors want their franchisees to be committed, personally and financially, to the success of their units. But they also want them to have enough money in reserve to be able to weather hard times, either during the start-up phase or during an uncontrollable economic downturn.

The Least Important Traits

The following traits were judged to be irrelevant to a franchisee's potential for success by most of the franchisors who replied to the survey. Some of them may surprise you.

Experience Working for a Big Company. Nearly 85 percent of the respondents said this trait had nothing to do with whether a franchisee could be successful in their system (in comparison, only 2 percent rated this trait as critical). While most franchisors have a number of franchisees who have bailed out of corporate life (or been euphemistically "outplaced"), they don't place much importance on this background.

Previous Experience in the Franchisor's Field.   Most of the franchisors surveyed downplayed the importance of experience in their line of business. In fact, over the years we have seen many franchisors who prefer to deal with franchisees who have no experience in their field. They feel that it is easier to train a novice than it is to *retrain* someone with preexisting ideas and habits that may be contrary to those of the franchisor.

Prior Business Ownership.   This trait was posed as both a positive and a negative (e.g., "Are franchisees who have previously owned their own business more likely to be successful as a franchisee?" and "Are franchisees who have *not* previously owned their own business more likely to be successful as a franchisee?"). Perhaps surprisingly, neither condition rated very highly among franchisors. With the obvious exception of conversion franchisees, franchisors are neither seeking out people who have owned their own businesses, nor are they systematically excluding these people. They feel that some level of business experience can be helpful, but the degree of experience is far less important in the development of a successful franchisee than, for example, an eagerness to learn and an ability to follow directions.

Personal Situation.   Middle-aged, married men with families as franchisees are usually regarded as being responsible individuals with vested interests in succeeding (i.e., to support their families). However, respondents to this survey indicated that age, sex, marital status and family situation mean little when it comes to predicting future franchisee success. The percentages of "irrelevant" as a choice for these four topics were as follows: age, 59 percent; sex, 79 percent; marital status, 71 percent; family status, 62 percent. These questions were not qualified; for example, the question simply inquired if the sex of a franchisee matters, *not* if the franchisor preferred males over females or vice versa.

Financial Acumen.   Did you often doze off during Accounting 101? Not to worry. More than 77 percent of the franchisors in our survey judged this characteristic to be either irrelevant or only somewhat important to a franchisee's success. Some knowledge of basic accounting and reporting conventions can be helpful, but whatever financial routines are needed will likely be taught by

the franchisor; standardized accounting, banking and other financial procedures will be part of the operating system provided. In general, franchisors are
looking for enthusiastic, committed people who learn quickly, not CPAs.

Other traits that the survey inquired about were judged to be neither ab-
solutely critical nor completely irrelevant. These include: general physical fit-
ness (although most franchisors would probably agree that the basic health of
a franchisee can make a big difference), creativity, participation in community
affairs, management experience (i.e., previously overseeing a staff, an outlet or
an entire business) or other specialized business skills and a willingness to
take risks.

Now that you know which traits are valued most by franchisors and which
mean relatively little, you should have a clearer picture of where you stand and
why you scored the way you did on the quiz. If you were disappointed with
your score, perhaps you could benefit from looking over the test questions
again; analyzing your responses as they compare to what you now know is important to a franchisor.

■ The Next Step—Making a Choice

Now that you have a better idea of how you rate—personally and profes-
sionally—as a prospective franchisee, the next step is to evaluate franchises
and then choose an organization. Of course, the franchisor you choose must
also choose you, but if you're pleased with your test score and you feel the
traits described in this chapter dovetail with your personality and experiences,
you have a good chance of appealing to many franchisors.

■ The Bottom Line on Franchising

A wealth of information about franchising can be garnered by studying its
bottom line. Since its inception, franchising has generated some truly impres-
sive statistics:

- Currently, 35 cents of every U.S. retail dollar are spent at a franchised
  business.
- By the year 2000, that total should increase to 55 cents.
- In the 1980s, franchising's annual sales more than doubled, from $336 bil-
  lion to an estimated $716 billion.

- By the year 2000, franchised sales are estimated to nearly double again and surpass $1 trillion per year.

- There are more than 542,000 U.S. franchise outlets, employing more than 7 million workers.

- It is estimated that a new franchised store opens in the United States every 16 minutes.

- According to the U.S. Department of Commerce, franchised outlets have a failure rate of less than 5 percent per year, while Dun & Bradstreet claims more than 50 percent of new businesses fail during their first five years.

■ ■ ■ ■ ■ ■ ■ ■ ■ ■ ■ ■ ■ ■ ■ ■ ■ ■ ■ ■

5

Buying a Business

There is a definite art to the business acquisition process. It consists of doing those extra things that keep you one step ahead of the competition, that make the difference between a deal and no deal, that turn an ordinary deal into an extraordinary deal.

The business acquisition process begins with techniques for finding a large number of business deals, and finding them before they come on the market, get listed with a broker or in a newspaper and attract potential competitors onto the scene to outbid you. These techniques collectively come under the rubric *the deal flow.*

■ How To Start the Deal Flow

The deal flow is a system for creating a stream of potential business acquisitions moving across your desk, to broaden your range of opportunities, to increase the number and quality of the deals and to make optimum use of your time. A deal flow is an ongoing parade of businesses marching across your desk in a quantity that allows you to pull out a few that meet your criteria. Most people who fail at buying businesses do so because they look at only one business and have to say yes or no: They have few other choices, no comparisons. In short, the idea is not to *find* yourself in the right place at the right time, but to *put* yourself in front of an endless deal flow.

The purpose of a deal flow is to generate many high-quality leads, which accomplishes three things. First, more choices mean a higher probability of finding a deal that matches your criteria. Second, practice improves your analytical skills, since each deal in your deal flow teaches you new questions to ask on all deals you are investigating. Third, each not-quite-right deal helps you refine your criteria.

A strong positive deal flow also has the side benefit of reducing your buyer remorse. Most people experience regret after making major purchases: "Maybe I shouldn't have bought that one." "I spent too much money." If you have done a good job of studying the market and your needs, and if you looked at a lot of candidates, you are likely to have fewer regrets.

There are, however, dangers in a strong positive deal flow. You can become very good at analyzing deals and finding reasons to say no. Obviously, the more you say no, the more deals you get to see. If you say yes, you have to do a thorough investigation, and that takes more time and effort. The danger is that you may overanalyze facts and figures and turn down too many deals. That, in turn, translates into fewer and lower-quality leads: Referrers will lose interest in you; finders will feel they are wasting their time. It's often called *paralysis by analysis*.

You can go into information overload and get bogged down in the sheer number of deals. Here I can help. I'll show you a system of ever-finer sieves you can use to quickly sort good deals from bad deals.

■ How To Build a Positive Deal Flow

I have helped dozens of people buy businesses, and typically the ones who come up with the best deals and the best terms have regularly applied strong positive deal flow techniques. If you have only limited funds (have you ever met anyone with *un*limited funds?), put them into developing a strong positive deal flow rather than into the back end of the acquisition process. With the right deal, you stand a good chance of needing less cash to close.

Below are numerous sources of a strong positive deal flow. The artistic element must be brought into play: Use your imagination to make a list of every person who might give you a lead to your targeted business. Then methodically work your list.

- your own company
- business broker
- printers

- newspaper advertisements
- the *Wall Street Journal*
- newspaper back issues
- brokers
- accountants
- attorneys
- suppliers
- salespeople and manufacturer reputation
- insurance agents
- SBA liquidation officers
- executive secretaries of trade associations
- customers
- real estate books
- buyer brokers
- bankruptcies
- corporate partners
- your own ads
- knocking on doors

Your Own Company

Insider buyouts are becoming commonplace. Look first at your own division, plant or group. Look for clues to management discontent or headaches. Is it a close match with the rest of the company, or is it in an "alien" industry? Does it regularly miss profitability targets? Is it saddled with unneeded controls or costs from outside? Is it simply a small tree in a large forest, unable to get the room it needs to grow? Ask the same questions about other divisions.

How do you find out if management will consider a buyout? Remember, insider buyouts are in the normal range of business transactions currently, and you can expect to be taken seriously. You need to approach the question with due regard to both formal and informal corporate hierarchies and procedures. Find someone in the organization who might be favorably disposed to the idea of an insider buyout, who would be willing to act as your sponsor. Then approach that person in an offhand fashion, such as by a request to "run an idea past you." Present the question in a nonthreatening way, perhaps as one of a series of choices: sell off some assets, scale down operations, sell to outsiders, sell to insiders, hire more specialized managers. *Many of the best deals come from this category. Don't overlook it!*

Business Brokers

Business brokers can be a good source of leads, depending on how you use them.

There are three levels of intermediaries in business deals. *Business opportunity brokers* are what most people mean when they speak of business brokers. These are people who work on deals priced generally up to $1 million. They can be found in the yellow pages under "Business Brokers" or similar entries and through newspaper ads. *Business intermediaries* put together deals in the range of $1 million to $20 million. They are also listed under "Business Brokers," but their names often sound more like law firms ("Smith and Jones") than trade names ("Businesses Unlimited"). Ask your banker, lawyer and accountant for the best introductions. *Investment bankers* work in the rarefied atmosphere of deals above $20 million. They are best approached through professionals.

The first leads you produce through a business opportunity broker, especially one who works with deals under $1 million will usually be mediocre. That's because those priced below that mark usually do not reach a broker until the owners have exhausted all the "normal" (and confidential) means of selling the business on their own.

You are not after the stale leads on the business opportunity broker's printed fliers. You want the leads she develops with you in mind, or the ones about which she calls you to say, "George from our office has an appointment at two o'clock tomorrow to list a business that fits your criteria perfectly, and I wanted you to be the first person to look at it." It will pay you to visit all of the good business opportunity brokers early on. They'll do more than increase your deal flow if you take the time to give them your criteria up front and keep in frequent contact with them.

The business opportunity brokerage is in its infancy, and there are few standards to go by. There are many first-rate business opportunity brokers, and they run their brokerages with the highest standard of ethics. Beware though— there are several of the other kind. The business opportunity broker who wants to charge you an up-front fee to review your financials or list you with his company as a buyer is not acting in a reputable fashion. Almost all business opportunity brokers work for the seller, and to charge both buyer and seller a fee or commission would be unusual. Evaluate these people very carefully.

Many of the best go-betweens have gravitated toward the business intermediary level, leaving the business priced below $1 million to be handled by the business opportunity brokers. But the good go-betweens are out there, and if your target market is below this range, you'll just have to search more diligently. The best way to find one is from a referral.

Before you deal with any brokers or business intermediaries, check them out thoroughly. *Get references from both buyers and sellers who have dealt with them* and call or visit these references. Call real estate brokers and ask if they can recommend a business broker or business intermediary and then mention the name of the one you are investigating. Call your banker and do the same. Call the Better Business Bureau or the chamber of commerce and see if they can give you a reading. Call the court clerk's office and see if that intermediary has been involved in many lawsuits. Once you are satisfied, then begin dealing in earnest with the go-between.

How To Use a Broker.   If you buy a business through a business opportunity broker, be aware that you should not normally use the broker as the negotiator for the entire deal. Business deals are not like real estate, where the discovery of the deal is 90 percent and communication between the parties is 10 percent. In the purchase of a business, with so many different aspects requiring open discussions (employees, suppliers, promissory notes, outside lenders, stockholders and so forth), much information has to be traded accurately and in a spirit of candor. If you are constantly going through third parties, the transfer of information is slowed and distorted.

For the same reason, attorneys and accountants shouldn't be allowed to do the entire deal, either. The two principals have to be working together. If it is a corporate deal, the two sets of teams have to negotiate the deal. So if you have a broker involved, thank her for putting the parties together, encourage her to pick up additional information not easily found, assure her about the commission and gently ease her out of the mainstream of the negotiating process.

Obviously, the broker needs to be kept informed of how the transaction is progressing, but she should not be allowed to run interference between the parties. There will be times when you will need her to act as arbitrator or conciliator in some ticklish spot, so don't cut the broker out entirely, but as a rule of thumb, do most of the negotiations yourself.

Printers

Printers are a great source of information about businesses for sale. What one line of business has customers in every other line of business? What one business owner knows when your business is going strong or drastically falling off? And what one business owner gets to read the major business news before the public? The printer, of course. Lawyers and accountants can give you many leads, but printers, who don't get called on as frequently, will give you leads to businesses that few other people know are for sale. They are bound by fewer confidentiality restrictions and can give you more insight into the prospects of the business. In short, you'll probably have a higher "hit ratio" with leads from printers.

Get to know a few printers, ask the right questions, and you'll find they can be a direct source of finding good businesses for sale. Wouldn't a direct mail campaign to printers or advertising in the printing magazines be a fitting way to create some of your deal flow?

Newspaper Advertisements

Just as owners of smaller businesses wait until the last minute to list with a broker, they also will not start the process with an ad in the newspaper. So, by the time an ad reaches the newspaper, it is likely that a number of people have already rejected it. It might say something, but it may also be an opportunity, since the business could be so highly specialized that only someone like you would understand it and see the real opportunities. Be your own judge.

You should respond to newspaper ads so you can gather data on the range of deals available, but don't expect an answer to your response. Many advertisers are just testing the salability of a business they are not ready to sell. Or they want to see who is interested and will screen carefully anyone to whom they send information. Many letters are just ignored. However, once in a while you will find a little gem in the paper, so don't ignore the ads.

Here is an example of a very successful advertisement that CEM ran in its monthly newsletter, *The Entrepreneurial Manager's Newsletter:*

WANTED: BUSINESS TO START OR BUY!

The son of one our New York CEO Club members is seeking to start or buy a business. If you know of a situation that fits this description please contact:

David Valluzzo
Vice President
DCG Precision Manufacturing Corp.
9 Trowbridge Drive
Bethel, CT 06801
203/743-5525
203/791-1737 Fax

David has an exceptionally broad background and diverse interests. His primary criteria for this new opportunity are its profit-making potential and its return on investment capital. Being single and in his early thirties, David can travel extensively or relocate anywhere in the world. He has been the chief financial officer of a business that grew from a few million dollars in annual sales to one that is expected to produce about ten times those sales this year. He has a strong analytical background and is excellent with computer and management information systems. He holds an MBA in finance from New York University.

While David is willing to be a partner in a much larger business, he is primarily seeking a business he can own and operate. He has just under $1 million of equity capital to invest in the right situation and access to five times more capital if necessary.

The ideal business would have a long history of profitability and owners who seek to retire in the next few years. The business would have exceptional growth opportunities in a rapidly expanding industry with a need to strengthen the finance area to cope with the growth. It would have between 10 and 100 employees and require strong analytical leadership to prosper.

If you know of a situation that fits this description, please contact David directly. There are no fees involved, and brokers will be protected.

The Wall Street Journal

The Thursday edition contains the greatest concentration of businesses for sale. Although newspaper ads generally are not the best source of businesses for sale, the *Journal* is too expensive for all but the most highly priced companies. The *Journal* also has less-costly regional editions. The smallest one is in Texas, and it is about 10 percent of the national circulation. You'll have to procure more than one regional edition to get 100 percent of the opportunities. You may want to also get its sister publication, the *National Business Employment Weekly.* It is expensive, but it contains all of *The Wall Street Journal*'s regional advertisements.

There's also the "Businesses for Sale" columns in *Success* and *Inc.* magazines. Since these magazines are monthlies they probably won't be in a hurry to sell. You will find more franchise offerings in *Entrepreneur* magazine, which is another good source.

Newspaper Back Issues

If you read the back issues of business and local periodicals, you will find news of who bought whom several months ago. Why would you want that information? One of the insider tricks in the business acquisition business is based on the infrequently considered fact that a major acquisition is often followed by a divestiture of unwanted divisions. Many management LBOs (leveraged buyouts) happen this way. The smaller division operating within a larger parent may not have gotten the attention it needed, or might have been stifled by corporate policy. When a new owner comes along, the small unprofitable division may be sold to raise cash for the corporate till. And it's not just unprofitable divisions that are divested.

While you're looking through old newspapers in your local library, ask about a little directory called *Who Owns Whom: The Directory of Corporate Affiliations,* published by National Register Publishing Company. Check through the list of subsidiaries to find those in your target area.

Divestitures can be some of the sweetest deals around. Management is often so glad to get rid of a headache it is willing to take back some of the financing (paper) at favorable terms. The amount of financing the seller takes back might be comparatively high, since the sales price of the small division might be inconsequential compared to the seller's annual budget.

In addition, think what the divestiture can mean in the realm of local politics. There is almost hysteria about local businesses being gobbled up by distant corporate raiders. Couple that with a potential loss of jobs to the local economy if the company consolidates the local plant, sells it off to another distant corporation or closes the doors in order to cut costs. If you have seen any of these happen in your own area, you know what I mean. Many localities are only too quick to grant loans, tax abatements, free land in municipal industrial parks and other incentives to keep businesses in town.

Management guru Peter F. Drucker, in his book *Innovation and Entrepreneurship* (Harper & Row, 1985), gives another reason back issues of newspapers may be a fertile source of deals. He suggests that hypergrowth companies usually experience an equally hyper need for cash in their early years. Thus, headlines two or three years old often presage financial difficulties today. Look for headlines in your fields of interest. Back issues of trade magazines can do the same thing.

Bankers

Bankers are not usually active participants until the deal has been negotiated and somebody wants financing. However, bankers are quite often in the inner circle of advisers for small businesses and will know when a business is for sale, sometimes before other professional advisers.

You should work with commercial loan officers (be sure to get at least to the level of a vice president or the head of a department), branch managers, executive vice presidents and presidents. In larger banks, you may not be able to get in touch with the president or an executive vice president, but why not investigate the banks that have only one or two branches?

You have to check out thoroughly whatever leads you are given. Bankers will tell you about profitable businesses for sale, and about the ones facing foreclosure, but they won't tell you which is which. You have to find that out for yourself. By the way, a business that is in trouble is not necessarily a bad deal, and vice versa.

Attorneys

Attorneys are also in the inner circle of advisers for most businesses. Look for attorneys who practice heavily in business and corporate law. Some can be found from their ads in the yellow pages. Others can be found by calling divorce or real estate attorneys (or anyone who doesn't practice business law) and asking for referrals. Check with bankers and small business owners for referrals, too.

Accountants

Outside accountants are the innermost circle of advisers for most small businesses. They work on the books 12 months a year, help with the tax return and see their clients many times during the year to talk about business. They know which businesses are for sale. They should be contacted early and often. Accountants who advise small businesses can be located in much the same way as attorneys—through bankers and business attorneys. Business (especially its professional advisers) is one big fraternity.

Suppliers

Let's say you're in a highly competitive business. Your customers are other businesses. The owner of one of your larger customers is getting ready to retire. He will either sell to an outsider or just liquidate and go out of business.

What's your stake? If your customer goes out of business, you have just lost a chunk of your profits. If your customer sells out to someone who is used to dealing with your competitor, you lose again. So what will you do? You will try to stay on top of your industry and make sure you know when your customers are for sale. You may even be willing to loan some of your hard-earned money to help someone buy your customer's business, just to keep the account. Besides, you know whose sales are doing what; you know how old your customers' owners are; you know who is getting fed up with the business and who is getting ready to retire. If you keep your ear to the ground, you are an excellent source of information about businesses for sale.

Salespeople and Manufacturers' Representatives

When a pharmacist was looking for a drugstore to buy, the ethical drug salesman who supplied his boss's store gave him leads to about a half-dozen drugstores for sale, one of which he eventually bought.

Just as the supplier does not want to lose his customers, neither does the supplier's commissioned salesperson or manufacturer's representative. And since the salespeople are in the customers' stores or plants frequently, they have a finger on the pulse of the marketplace. They are one of the best "underground" sources of information about businesses for sale. In fact, salespeople and manufacturers' representatives know so much about how well or how poorly a business is doing, or about the health and enthusiasm of the owner, that they may know *before the owner does* when a business is for sale.

Insurance Agents

Insurance agents have gotten a bum rap over the years. But talk to many small business owners and you will discover that their own insurance agent is often a trusted adviser. It's the "other" insurance agents they don't like. The insurance agent is perhaps advising about health insurance, pensions, disability insurance, fire coverages and other year-to-year needs of the business. The life insurance agent, as opposed to the property-casualty agent, may also be advising on pensions, buy-sell agreements among co-owners and a multitude of ways for the business owner to get money out of his or her corporation for personal needs. As such, insurance agents may have an inside track on when a business is for sale. Since they see so many businesses, they have exposure to a wide marketplace. They make their living by knowing their clients well, and they can be an excellent source of information for you.

SBA Liquidation Officers

When a Small Business Administration guaranteed or direct loan turns sour, it is turned over to the liquidation officer, whose job it is to try and recoup the losses. Many businesses on the bad loan list are for sale. To identify them, contact the liquidation officer in your local area and the one at the SBA in Washington (202/205-6600; 800/827-5722 Answer Desk).

Visit the liquidation officer in person. This will demonstrate your commitment more effectively than a phone call. Send a follow-up note after the meeting. None of this paper is thrown away. Remember, bureaucrats eat, sleep and drink paper. And you don't want to be forgotten.

Be sure to also visit the SBA's management assistance officers in your area. These are counselors to troubled businesses. The liaison officers in the smaller SBA regional offices also perform these duties and should be visited. When contacting these officials, be aware that their work with clients is confidential, so ask indirectly. For example, ask if they have any clients who are currently seeking buyers, or who might be sometime soon.

There are numerous other SBA services you may find helpful. The college-run Small Business Development Centers (SBDC) and the Service Corp of Retired Executives (SCORE) are both excellent. The list here is endless and would require another book to access. But don't overlook it.

Executive Secretaries of Trade Associations

Trade associations in just about every industry are headed by a president and vice president elected from among the membership. Many also have a position called executive secretary. This person is the top paid executive in the association—the person who runs the day-to-day operations.

The executive secretary is the person the president calls on to find out what is usually done in a given situation or which committee handles what. The members also call him for all types of help. The executive secretary is paid to help the members and to know what's up, so he is a natural person for members to contact when they want to sell their business. He is also the person who sees most business sale ads *before* they appear in the organization's publications.

The *Directory of Directories* and the *Encyclopedia of Associations,* both published by Gale Research in Detroit and available at your library, contain listings of most of the major trade associations in the country. (See Appendix.) You will probably find two or three dozen associations in or near your field, many of which have state chapters or affiliates. Each probably has an executive director or secretary who will talk with you, since you might become a member. You might want to acquire these two directories from Gale as they are excellent.

Another innovative way to use a trade association is to attend its meetings and conferences. Be sure to include associations in the industries that supply your target industry. Your goal is to rub elbows with as many people as possible during the conference, passing along the word that you have a management team that specializes in turnarounds and acquisitions. You could also run an advertisement in the trade show newspapers. Few people are doing this, so it gives you an opportunity to find some of the better businesses for sale before everyone else does. It's usually the more outgoing people who attend conventions and continuing education seminars, and they are excellent sources of acquisition information.

Customers

Just as suppliers may know which businesses are for sale, your customers can lead you to their own suppliers that may be on the block. Businesses have a big stake in seeing that major suppliers stay in business. Contact these sources through trade associations or directly.

Real Estate Brokers

Most real estate brokers are a little overawed by the details, paperwork and investigations intrinsic in business sales. There are a few who work in this area, but their depth of understanding varies. Real estate brokers involved in business brokerage are usually reputable, ready to admit their lack of knowledge and willing to get necessary information. They are good at generating leads.

Buyer's Broker

Business brokers normally represent the seller. However, there is nothing illegal or immoral about a business broker representing the buyer. Since his incentive would be to secure the highest price, you will not want to hire a business broker on a percentage basis to help you buy a business. You'll want to pay the business broker by the hour to bring you deals or perhaps by the number of qualified deals he presents. Incentive compensation could also be based on the improvement in sales price obtained by the broker.

Work closely with the broker, explaining your criteria in depth, and give plenty of feedback on any and all deals you turn down, whatever the compensation arrangement. Since brokers themselves have to develop a good deal flow to keep their businesses going, their flow can be a shortcut to your own deal flow.

Bankruptcies

Just because a business is in bankruptcy is no reason for it to close. Chapter 11, for instance, is used to continue the business while legally keeping creditors away. Bankruptcy doesn't necessarily mean the business itself is bad (although you may want to investigate). A weekly newsletter called the *National*

Bankruptcy Reporter gives information on large bankruptcies. It's available through Andrews Publications in Westtown, Pennsylvania, but the price is stiff—about $1,800 a year, $900 for a half year. Your friendly local bankruptcy attorney or local law library may have copies you can review. (See Appendix.)

Another source is the local bankruptcy judge. Let bankruptcy judges and trustees know you "have turnaround teams available" and are interested in buying businesses. You might also find it challenging to seek a position as a bankruptcy trustee for a company in order to help turn it around or liquidate it. Several famous venture capitalists started this way.

Also plan to visit the clerk's office of the local bankruptcy court to check for Chapter 11 filings a couple of months old. These are financially troubled companies that have sought the court's protection from creditor lawsuits while they try to turn things around. After several months they may have gotten worse. As an outsider you can perform miracles: You can buy assets free of creditors and usually at bargain prices. Insiders, on the other hand, need to find some way to deal with the mountain of debt they have built up before they can bring the company out of bankruptcy.

If you wait until the company closes its doors, you can get it for a song, but by then the customers and most valuable employees may have fled. You have to weigh for yourself whether the low price is worth what you must give up. But don't overlook the bankruptcy court as a place to cherry-pick a few good assets for the business you acquire outside bankruptcy. Watch the legal notices and newspaper classifieds for auction sales.

Another source of information is the credit report newsletter published by credit bureaus or other credit reporting agencies in most large cities. Locate your local one through your chamber of commerce or your attorney. These newsletters report bankruptcies and lawsuits filed locally. Also, if you find a certain company is regularly getting sued, it may point toward an owner anxious to bail out, perhaps at a bargain price.

Corporate Partners

Several large companies encourage entrepreneurs both inside and outside their corporate hierarchies. Prime among them recently have been 3M and General Electric. They continually create new inventions and businesses that they cannot cash in on themselves, so they sell or license them to small companies. Sometimes it is done in the form of whole operating divisions, and more often as just raw technology. Watch the business press for clues as to who is spinning off opportunities. Contact these companies and any other large companies in your field to see if they have any interest in licensing. Some companies may have licensing departments, but it pays to make friends with the switchboard operator and the head of research and development (R&D) to find out who is really the knowledgeable person.

Your Own Ads

Some promoters in the real estate field suggest putting ads in the newspaper: "We buy real estate. Call Jim." If you do the same for a business, your ad should be longer. Tell something about yourself, and describe the type of business you're targeting. Sound professional. Not many have used this technique with businesses, but there's no reason why it wouldn't work. Try it and then improve it each time. Rather than run it only under "Business to Buy," try the category called "Capital to Invest." You could begin by explaining that you'd be willing to invest in the right situation. Often those are the same people who later begin reading the "Business Wanted to Buy" section.

Knocking on Doors

Visit businesses in your targeted industry and talk to the owners. How do you go about knocking on doors? If the business is retail, visit as if you were a customer. Browse around and keep alert. Are the shelves well stocked, or is there a lot of dusty, shopworn or dated inventory? Is the cash register constantly ringing, or do the salesclerks sit around reading? What is the attitude of the personnel? Are they anxious to help, or sloppy? Little things such as these can be clues to how well the business is doing and whether or not it might be for sale. Time your visit for less busy hours. For manufacturing concerns, you can learn a lot by sitting outside the gate at shift change, looking and listening for employee attitudes and so forth.

To learn who the owner is, check in the city directory or just call the store and ask. For nonretail establishments, consult the *Thomas Register* (of American manufacturers) or call the company directly.

Be businesslike and courteous when talking to the owner. Demonstrate your knowledge about her industry, and explain you are looking to acquire an operating business. Is it possible that she might know of some businesses for sale? The owner probably won't mention her own business unless she is particularly anxious to sell, but she will talk about others in an effort to determine whether you are really someone who knows the business or if you're just a competitor seeking inside information. Once she trusts you, there'll be plenty of time to find out whether her own business is for sale.

PART TWO

■

The Entrepreneurial Process

6

The Business Plan

The first task when buying or starting a business is to prepare a business plan. This puts all the information down in one place on paper for everyone to read and understand. It's a road map for you to go from one place to another. You could attempt an automobile trip from Los Angeles to New York without a map, relying only on road signs, but would you? Neither should you attempt an even more difficult task without working out the problems on paper first.

■ It All Begins with a Plan

It is well established that you can't raise money without a business plan. If you try to, the financial source will say, "Come back and see us again when your plan is ready."

Every company that has ever existed has had to start with some kind of plan. Maybe it's called a feasibility study or maybe it's called *the deal,* but it is a business plan by any name. One of the best ways to prepare a business plan is to remove yourself from your own business. Step back and take an objective look. One good way to gain this kind of objectivity is to examine other people's business plans before you go to work on your own. Look critically at what is there and try to figure out what is missing. Later, you should examine your own plan in the same way.

No entrepreneur or CEO confronted with the need to create a business plan ever said, "Oh Goody! I can't wait to write it. This will be fun!" No one wants to write one, and everyone tries to find a shortcut to the process. Thousands of CPAs and consultants make their living by charging $5,000 to $20,000 to write business plans for other people. It's a good business and you just might want to consider it as an option among the businesses you are considering.

Two of my books published by Simon & Schuster have been perennial best-sellers in this narrow field for the past two decades:

- *How to Prepare and Present a Business Plan* (contains three actual plans for a restaurant, a computer company and a solar energy company).

- *How to Write a Winning Business Plan* (contains the plans that launched three famous U.S. companies: Storage Technology, *Venture* magazine and Shopsmith).

In addition, my association, The Center for Entrepreneurial Management, Inc., 180 Varick St., Penthouse, New York, NY 10014, 212/633-0060, offers companion information in audio and video cassettes with a 116-page work-book. I tell you all this because it would take a whole book to help you write this all-important document called the business plan.

That's the bad news. The good news is I'll tell you how they are read and analyzed in this chapter. Armed only with this information you'll be able to write one better, but it will be no easier to write.

■ How to Read a Business Plan

It's ironic that it usually takes ten months and $10,000 to create a business plan, but that it can be analyzed in just five minutes. Not in depth, but close enough to make a go-no go decision. I say don't fight this inevitable result be-cause it has been the same for the past three decades; instead, go with the flow and adjust your plan to appeal to the five-minute reader.

I conducted numerous in-depth interviews with bankers and venture capital-ists and others in the financial community, to discover how a financial source usually spends this precious five minutes. Each source prides itself on its so-phistication in analyzing investment opportunities. Almost everyone, my study revealed, analyzed the plans in about the same way, using the following steps (less than a minute is invested in each step):

Step 1. Determine the characteristics of company and industry.
Step 2. Determine the terms of the deal.
Step 3. Read the latest balance sheet.
Step 4. Determine the caliber of the people in the deal.

Step 5. Determine what is different about this deal.
Step 6. Give the plan a once-over lightly.

■ Step One: Determine the Characteristics of Company and Industry

A single venture capitalist rarely excels in every industry, just as a single entrepreneur cannot manage with equal skill in diverse industries. Thus, each venture capitalist has preferred areas for investment. The venture capitalist's area of expertise is developed over the years and is based upon past successes. Some like computers; some like high technology, others low technology; others like consumer goods; and still others prefer publishing. Consequently, many potential investors may never read a business plan beyond step 1, regardless of the terms of the deal, if they have little interest in the industry. Fortunately, several good venture capital guidebooks exist that not only identify venture capital sources, but also highlight their industry preferences. The industry bible, *Pratt's Guide to Venture Capital Sources* (SDC Publishing, 212/765-5311), indexes 800 venture firms by company name and industry and includes articles on the state of that industry. Look for *Pratt's* at the library. (See Appendix for a listing of venture capital associations and networks.)

Is This Industry Hot?

Every potential investor also factors the current glamour of the specific industry into the analysis. Are there any larger publicly traded companies in the same industry? If so, how high is the stock price/earning multiple (P/E ratio) of these firms? Or, better yet, is there a larger company that is extremely successful in this industry? How well has it done? Companies find it easier to raise funds when another company has pioneered successfully. For example, in the computer industry, Data General Corporation could point to Digital Equipment Corporation; in the consumer goods industry, many smaller companies have pointed to Avon Products or Alberto-Culver. A specialty chemical company that eventually failed, Lanewood Laboratories, raised $500,000 based on a business plan that pointed to Lestoil. Without Lestoil's prior success, Lanewood would never have raised money. The BLT Company carwash gas station successfully raised more than $1 million just after Robo-Wash went public with an initial offering. This is the business plan in the back of my book *How to Start, Finance and Manage Your Own Small Business* (Simon & Schuster, 1988). However, BLT went belly-up in less than two years. It would never have raised a penny if Robo-Wash had not preceded it.

Industry glamour rises and falls much like the length of women's skirts. Ten years ago, the glamour field was electronics, followed by franchising, and then by computers. Then it was energy and genetic engineering, tomorrow it may be superconductivity. Despite the obvious problems with financial fads, everyone accepts them as a reality. They exist and they do make a difference; if one's industry is momentarily glamorous, one's chances of securing funds suddenly increase.

Investors must hope to get out of their investments eventually. Thus, glamour is important. Investors must become liquid again to be able to invest in the next business, as that is their business, so determining the salability (glamour) of an industry before investing is crucial.

After examining and evaluating the industry, the potential investor will categorize the individual company within the industry based on the following criteria:

- annual sales
- profit or loss for last year
- number of employees
- market share
- degree of technology
- geographic location
- types of products

Highlighting these items in a front-page summary of the business plan saves the reader time.

With these facts, the investor will soon be able to determine whether the company is a suitable investment. Is it too large or small? Is it too far away? There are many good reasons for not making an investment; venture capitalists are seldom, if ever, faulted for the investments not made. They are more often and more intensely criticized for the ones they did select. The sequence in step 1 is first to check the industry, then to check the company.

■ Step Two: Determine the Terms of the Deal

How much of a company is being sold for what price is called the *terms of the deal*. The peripheral issue is the form (debt or equity) of the deal being offered. Many venture firms prefer convertible debt (or debt with warrants) to a straight equity deal. Their profit-seeking structure may require the venture firm to generate annual income to pay current overhead in addition to the capital gains expected from the capital portfolio. Naturally, these firms would prefer interest-bearing debt to help cover this overhead, and a few of them will discourage deals that do not satisfy this basic requirement. In these cases, form is not a peripheral issue; but in the majority of cases the more substantive issue of "how much for how much" is of more concern. Accordingly, a well-done business plan informs the reader of the following financial items on the first page.

Again, try to save the reader time by including these additional items on the summary page.

- percentage of company being sold (after dilution)
- total price for this percentage (per share figures also included)
- minimum investment (number of investors sought)
- total valuation (after the placement) being placed on the company
- terms of the investment:

  —common stock

  —preferred stock

  —debt with warrants

  —convertible debentures

  —subordinated convertible debt

  —straight debt

Following is a more complete explanation of these last six terms.

Common stock. Common stock is the term used to describe the documents that represent the value on the books of the business. When the funds are initially put into a company, common stock is known as capital stock. These certificates of common stock describe the ownership of the company. Common stock offerings are the most basic form of security issued in a private placement and offer the investor no special benefits or preferences. Common stock is generally selected if a company wishes to preserve its Subchapter S status under the Internal Revenue Code, which would be jeopardized if a new class of preferred stock were authorized.

Preferred stock. This special category of stock is treated better than simple common stock in some ways. Most of the time, preferred stock has certain advantages, such as guaranteed dividends or prior rights in a liquidation, and it is a separate category above common stock. Preferred stock can be structured to offer a number of advantages to an investor, such as convertibility into common stock, dividend and liquidation preference over common stock, antidilution protection, mandatory or option redemption schedules, and special voting rights and preferences. This gives the investor a variety of rights that the founders, typically the holders of the common stock, don't have. But at the same time, these preferred stock rights don't typically prejudice the interest of the company.

Debt with warrants. The debt of a company is simply an obligation to repay a certain amount of money over a certain period of time at an agreed-upon rate. In the simplest terms, it's a loan. Some loans are risky, and a high interest rate is not enough to make the loan financially attractive. Hence, stock warrants are attached to the debt to "sweeten" the investment. Warrants are rights to buy shares of common stock at a fixed price within a specified time period. If the price of the common stock rose above the predetermined stock warrant price within the time period, the holder of the warrant could exercise the warrant.

If, for instance, the warrant was at $3 per share and the stock was trading at $5 per share, a holder of the warrant could opt to exercise the warrant. A holder of 1,000 warrants could buy stock from the company for $3,000 and supposedly resell the same stock for $5,000, less appropriate commissions. Hence, a warrant is like a stock option, and it has some value. The value is only realized after the warrants are exercised and the stock is sold. Warrants enable an investor to buy common stock without sacrificing the preferred position of a creditor, as would be the case if only convertible debentures were issued. The exercise of the warrant brings fresh cash into the company, the amount of which depends on the number of warrants issued and the exercise price per share.

A classic example of a debt with warrants-type of investment occurred in the mid-1960s. Fred Fideli of the Worcester-based firm, State Mutual Life Assurance Company, traveled to Chicago to evaluate a growing chain of hamburger stands. Although only 100 units were operating at that time, after visiting about 75 of them, Fideli offered a loan of $750,000 with an interest rate of 7½ percent to this business, then headed by the legendary entrepreneur, Ray Kroc. In addition, to sweeten the financial attractiveness of this loan, Fideli obtained warrants to purchase 20 percent of the common stock of the hamburger chain.

About ten years later, State Mutual had received full repayment of its loan, exercised the warrants on the company and sold the stock in the public market. Rumor has it that this conservative life insurance company realized about $12 million profit on this loan.

Convertible debentures. A debenture is a loan. The convertible feature allows the debt holder to convert the remaining outstanding debt into stock. For instance, a five-year note for $500,000 at 10 percent simple annual interest, payable monthly, is a form of debt. The convertible feature would allow the note holder to convert any remaining debt into common stock at a specific price.

A simple debt instrument or a loan would be paid off at a steady rate over the life of the loan. In this example, a five-year loan of $500,000 would disappear at the end of the fifth year. About half of it, or $250,000, would still be due after 30 months with 30 months left to pay. When and if it became attractive, a convertible note holder could trade in the remainder of the debt for common stock at a predetermined price. The difference between this technique and debt with warrants is simple. Under convertible debts, the note holder might not recover all the loan before purchasing the stock. In the case of debt with warrants, all the debts must be repaid and, in addition, the note holder is given warrants that he may or may not exercise. Today, more venture capitalists prefer a debt with warrants deal rather than convertible debt.

Subordinated convertible debt. This is a special class of debt. The adjective *subordinated* refers to the ranking of this debt as compared to other forms of debt in event of liquidation. Subordinated debt is usually senior to any equity but subordinated to any other debt, especially bank borrowing. In case of bankruptcy or liquidation, subordinated debt is paid after all other debts, usually including trade payables, are satisfied. The stockholders are traditionally the only group of investors with lower priority than holders of subordinated debts. The convertible feature remains the same as described above. The only difference between convertible debentures and subordinated convertible debentures is that the latter is also subordinated to other debt. Until converted, however, it offers a fixed rate of return and certain tax advantages (i.e., you can deduct interest payments). Many investors like the hedge that this type of security provides.

Following is a common ranking of rights in a bankruptcy:

1. certain IRS liens
2. secured creditors
3. unsecured creditors (trade payables)
4. subordinated debt
5. stockholders

Straight debt. This is simply a loan or debenture—an obligation to pay back an amount of borrowed funds at an agreed-upon rate over an agreed-upon period. There are two basic forms of straight debt: secured and unsecured. Secured debt is further backed up by an asset that is pledged to guarantee repayment. In the event of default, the secured lender could seize the pledged asset to recover the outstanding debt. A house mortgage is a good example of secured debt. Any debt without an asset pledged as collateral is unsecured.

The Remaining Terms of the Deal

Every business plan contains considerable detail, and the terms mentioned above only cover a few points of interest. You might also want to include the following points in summarizing the terms of the deal:

- How does the price per share of this placement compare with the founders' price per share?
- Are the founders reinvesting in this placement?
- What was the value of the company at the last placement and why has it changed?
- How will the new funds be used? Will they be used to repay old debts or to undertake new activities that, in turn, will increase profitability?

■ Step Three: Read the Latest Balance Sheet

A current balance sheet is usually located at the end of the written business plan, just before the appendix and future estimates or (pro forma) cash flow and income statements. The most current balance sheet is usually the first page of the financial exhibits, and it is often the *only* financial page glanced at during an initial reading of a business plan. This document exposes the company's history, whereas most other financial documents in the appendix describe the company's future hopes.

Much preferred to any pro forma analysis is a one-minute process for interpreting the balance sheet and income statement. (Merrill, Lynch publishes a 24-page brochure, *How to Read a Financial Report,* available at no cost at any branch office.) The following four-step process, which is used to read a balance sheet from the top down, offers most of the financial information needed to make a quick evaluation of the deal:

1. Determine liquidity.
2. Determine debt/equity structure.
3. Examine net worth.
4. Examine assets and liabilities.

Determine Liquidity

Check working capital or current ratio, each of which measures about the same thing. Working capital is equal to current assets minus current liabilities, while current ratio is current assets divided by current liabilities. Below is a typical balance sheet illustrating these relationships:

Cash	$ 50,000
Accounts receivable	200,000
Inventories	+250,000
Total current assets	$500,000
Accounts payable	$250,000
Notes payable (within one year)	75,000
Accrued expenses payable	100,000
Federal income tax payable	+ 25,000
Total current liabilities	$450,000

Working capital: $50,000 ($500,000–450,000)

Current ratio: +1.1 ($500,000/$450,000)

A firm's working capital should be positive, and the current ratio should be greater than 1. (Those two statements say the same thing in different words.) A current ratio closer to 2 indicates a more financially stable company. A company with less than $100,000 in working capital is generally tight on cash. A quick check will determine the firm's payroll. Relating payroll to cash (or working capital) will place the firm's needs for cash in a better perspective. For instance, if a firm with a balance sheet like the one above needs $100,000 per month for payroll, its cash is only two weeks of payroll, and its working capital is only half a month of payroll. This analysis indicates the firm's need for cash and is a fair indication of how well it is doing.

Determine Long-Term Debt/Equity Structure

The debt/equity ratio is equal to total debt divided by total equity. The ratio reveals how much credit a debt source (such as a bank) has already extended to the company. In addition, it offers insight into the remaining borrowing power of the company. A 3:1 debt/equity ratio, where a lender advances three dollars for every dollar, is a ballpark upper limit for this ratio. Seldom will debt sources advance three long-term debt dollars for every equity dollar in a small company. Consequently, a debt/equity ratio of 3:1 is rare, while a ratio of 1:1 usually indicates the company has some borrowing power remaining.

The numerator usually consists of long-term debt, such as bonds or mort-gages, and never includes current liabilities (due within one year), such as accounts payable. The denominator is tangible net worth or owner's equity at the time of the placement. This is not to be confused with the initial investment of the owners, which may have been made some time ago. Many times, small companies have unusually high (larger than one) debt/equity ratios. This often indicates that outside assets other than those on the company's balance sheet are securing the debt. A wealthy owner may have countersigned the bank note or pledged an asset in order to obtain more debt. The debt/equity ratio often generates clues to this discrepancy. In the above example, the debt/equity ratio is 2:3.

Examine Net Worth

The potential investor extracts from the balance sheet the amount of money initially invested in the firm, which is the initial capitalization provided by the founders. The cumulative profits (or losses) that are contained within the retained earnings offer another benchmark of the company's success to date. These two items added together algebraically determine a company's current net worth. Below is a typical balance sheet:

Long-term debt (current portion that is due this year is shown under current liabilities)	$100,000	line 1
Capital stock (initial capitalization)	+250,000	line 2
Retained earnings (profit or loss to date)	(100,000)	line 3
Owner's equity* (combines capitalization and retained earnings)	150,000	line 4

$$\frac{\text{Line 1}}{\text{Line 2} + \text{Line 3}} = \frac{\text{Debt}}{\text{Equity}} = \frac{\$100}{\$150} = .667 = \tfrac{2}{3}$$

A prospective investor interprets this information by noting that the founders began the company with $250,000 and have lost $100,000 since its inception. The company has a long-term, interest-bearing note that was proba-

---

*Owner's equity is what is put in to start the company plus or minus the earnings to date, which is equal to line 2 + line 3.

bly awarded when the company was founded and was based upon the initial capital of $250,000. After determining what, if anything, is offered as security for the long-term debt, an investor examines the footnotes to the balance sheet. *Many financial sources claim they begin the process of interpreting the financial sheet by reading the footnotes to the balance sheet!* However, due to the losses to date, the company probably has little remaining borrowing power. The investor will make a quick check to determine which assets (accounts receivable, inventory or fixed assets) are pledged to secure any of the debt. Free and unencumbered assets indicate more borrowing power.

The debt-to-worth ratio is only one factor to consider in determining a business's borrowing power. Other issues of concern to a lending source are the strength of any personal endorsements and the profitability of the business.

As a rule of thumb, a debt source will allow the following amounts of debt shown in column 2 to be secured against the assets shown in column 1.

Asset as It Appears on Balance Sheet	Percentage of Balance Sheet Value That Can Be Borrowed Against
Cash or marketable securities	100%
Accounts receivable	75–85% of those under 90 days (Percentage will depend on market value, not on book value)
Inventory	20–30%
Fixed assets	75% (Percentage will depend on market value, not book value)

Examine Assets and Liabilities

A potential investor will check to be sure all assets are real (tangible); then he or she will check liabilities to verify that debt is owed to outsiders, not to insiders (such as notes to stockholders). This determination hinges on the reputation of the accounting firm that prepared the financial statement. An unaudited, company-generated financial statement is seldom even interpreted because the investor needs some independent assurances that the financial reporting is accurate. Without this assurance, investors will undoubtedly downgrade the deal, at least during the initial reading. A report by a reputable CPA firm adds needed status to your financials.

By examining the asset categories, investors check to be sure soft assets (such as goodwill, patents or trade secrets, formulas or capitalized research and development) are not large or unreasonable. For some unexplained reasons, small companies often choose to capitalize research and development or organizational expenses rather than write them off during the period in which they occur. This practice is frowned upon by all potential investors because it distorts the balance sheet, impairs future earnings and is a sure sign of danger. If this "asset" is large, it can dampen an investor's interest.

Furthermore, entrepreneurs and friends and relatives of entrepreneurs often choose to make their initial investment in small companies as debt rather than equity. This makes them feel more secure because it offers some protection in the event of bankruptcy. But it scares away new investors, so you may want to clear this issue before you finalize your business plan. By making a quick check, a potential investor uncovers the identity of the company's creditors and the amount of debt.

In the initial reading of the business plan, potential investors are not probing the balance sheet in depth but are searching for red flags. Before an investment is consummated, they will analyze the balance sheet, income statement and pro formas in detail. But during the first glance, the balance sheet and the magnitude of last year's sales as shown on the profit-and-loss statement provide sufficient data to judge whether or not a more detailed financial investigation is warranted.

■ Step Four: Determine the Caliber of the People in the Deal

This step is the single most important element in a business plan. A potential investor begins by examining the reputations of the founders, board of directors, current investors and outside professionals (accountants, lawyers, bankers, consultants, directors). Unfortunately, this is a subjective area, and as such is open to a wide range of individual interpretations; what is good to some is not so good to others. Because it is subjective, opinions and assessments fluctuate dramatically.

Consequently, the reputations of *all* the individuals surrounding the business are of deep concern in securing additional funds. For start-up deals or for situations where the company is unknown to the potential investors, a number of questions are asked in order to determine management's abilities. This format is about the same for both internal and external businesses. However, internal venture teams are greatly assisted when the project directors are highly regarded by corporate management. Many times the *golden boy syndrome* becomes the crucial variable in approving new corporate funds.

Here are the issues.

- What is the track record of founders and managers, including where they worked and how well they performed in the past?
- How much experience does the inner management team possess? How long have the members worked together, and what degree of balance among marketing, finance and manufacturing is represented by the operating managers?
- Who is the financial person (or bank or accountant), and what are his or her credentials? (Potential investors prefer to deal with one strong, full-time financial type. They see this person as a caretaker for new funds.)

Potential investors usually know someone associated with the company (or someone who knows someone), and this person can be an important source of information for them. The insider can set the tone for the whole deal, regardless of his or her affiliations with the company. The company loses its identity, and the business plan becomes known as "John Smith's deal" around the office.

Most management teams include only their resumes in the business plan, but they are missing a gigantic area of opportunity. A Dallas CEO Club member who also belongs to the Dallas Presidential Advisory Council (PAC) put his deal over the top by including a list of fellow PAC members with his business plan. The group consists of a dozen CEOs of unrelated businesses who serve as a mutual board of advisers for one another. By including the list, he showed potential investors that he was already listening to outside advice. That strengthened his plan's appeal. Plus, investors could contact familiar names on the list for input on his management abilities (which they did).

■ Step Five: Determine What Is Different about This Deal

This difference can be the eventual pivotal issue on whether or not a specific venture capital firm chooses to invest. The same holds true for obtaining headquarters approval for internal venture management teams in larger companies.

Is there an unusual feature in the product? Does the company have a patent, an unusual technology, or a significant lead over competition? Is this a company whose critical skill rests in marketing, manufacturing, or finance? Does the company's strength match the skills needed to succeed in this industry? Or is there an imbalance? What is different about this company, and how much better are its products? These are the investor's chief concerns.

Does the company have the potential to open up a whole new industry, as Polaroid, Xerox, IBM, Digital Equipment Corporation, McDonald's and Hewlett-Packard did? Or is this a modest idea with limited future growth? Venture capitalists need a return of greater than ten times the initial investment just to stay even (one in ten succeeds). They are seldom intrigued with companies that hold a marginal advantage over competing firms or products. In essence, this is what Rooser Reeves has called the *unique selling proposition*: Good ideas or products that are better than others attract capital. Marginal improvements do not possess enough potential to offset the risks inherent in a new business venture.

■ Step Six: Give the Plan a Once-Over Lightly

A casual look at product literature, graphs, unusual exhibits, samples, letters of recommendation and letters of intent is the purpose of this last check. New opinions are seldom formed during the final minute, but the fact that everyone engages in this leafing-through process supports the argument for eye-catching enclosures. A product pasted on a page, a letter with a meaningful letterhead, or an unusual chart or two can extend the readership of a business plan.

After the final step, the analysis is over and the investors decide whether to obtain more information or to return the plan. Ninety-nine times out of a hundred, the deal is turned down. A few investors make phone calls at this stage, and then reject the deal after confirming a detail or two. But it is important to remember that deals are actually turned down during the first reading, even though the act of formal rejection may be postponed a few additional days.

■ The Plan Package

Most entrepreneurs assume that a positive relationship exists between time invested in reading the plan and the likelihood of obtaining capital. "If they would only read my plan," mumbles the unsuccessful entrepreneur, "they would be after me, not the other way around." With this goal in mind, and assuming the product is only as good as the package, many entrepreneurs invest considerable time and money developing impressive-looking leatherbound plans.

I conducted some tests to determine the method several dozen venture capitalists used to select a single business plan from a group of five to ten. Several deals were randomly placed on a table and the investors were asked to examine only the covers of the business plans before selecting which ones they would read first. The plans that received the most initial attention were not the ones with pretty covers; instead, the company name was most crucial. Next in importance was the geographical location of the company. The third element was the thickness of the plan; the shorter plans received more attention. The quality of the cover was the least important variable. In these tests, nothing else was revealed about any of the business plans other than what appeared on the cover. The position of the deals on the tables was random.

The next question I explored was, How can an entrepreneur increase the likelihood that a venture capitalist will read a business plan past the cover? Should the entrepreneur send it along in installments with the final chapter first, or should he or she send along a summary? In my research, I concluded that summaries and "miniplans" are not effective documents. A teaser summary that is not an integral part of the plan only delays the eventual reading of the entire plan, and the teaser is often vague or incomplete. It is much better to have the entire document available to every potential investor and to highlight the plan with a succinct and informative summary page as the first page of the business plan. Using the earlier road map analogy, would a minimap be sufficient to undertake a trip from San Francisco to Boston? When entrepreneurs tell me they have a mini-business plan, I always ask, "Where is the real one?" The miniplan is not only useless, it's actually a negative. You'd be better off without one, as you already created a doubt in my mind.

■ Delivery and Preselling Strategies

Two additional variables were uncovered that help to determine a plan's eventual reading, and, to a lesser extent, the likelihood that a venture capitalist will make an investment. The first is the method of dispatching the plan. The second is preselling, which precedes the plan. Entrepreneurs spend months preparing the plan, but only a few minutes deciding how to deliver it. Armed with a directory and a secretary, the naive entrepreneur follows the suicidal path of a blind mass mailing. This wastes everyone's time and the entrepreneur's money because this procedure never works.

Another bad approach is to make a personal visit with the business plan tucked under your arm. This humble, straightforward approach is like going to a doctor as an unreferred patient. Everyone asks, "Who sent you?" The key person is often away from the office or unable to see the visitor, who then begins to feel like an intruder.

The best method of delivering a business plan is through a third party. Unless the entrepreneur is already established and successful, a third-party referral adds credibility to the plan and increases the likelihood it will be read. Consultants, investors, bankers, lawyers, accountants or other entrepreneurs are all acceptable envoys as long as their reputations and liaisons with the venture capitalist are positive.

Preselling is another good way to ensure that your plan is read. If potential investors are told about the exciting company six months before the plan arrives and then about current developments each month for the intervening six months, they will be more receptive to reading the plan when it finally arrives. After all, *the best time to raise money is when it isn't needed.* The same holds for arousing potential investor interest. A well-managed company planning to expand will invest time in such preselling often and early. The preselling is as important as any aspect of the process.

The same person should both presell and eventually deliver the plan. With the company name and address and location clearly spelled out on the cover page, it should be hand-carried by a mutual friend to a select group of venture capitalists.

If the selection process seems depressing, remember that the two most successful venture capital deals in the Northeast were turned down a number of times before receiving a yes. In 1958, Digital Equipment Corporation (DEC) finally convinced American Research & Development to invest about $70,000. That investment today is worth several billion dollars.

A spin-off from DEC occurred in 1968 when three engineers in their twenties approached Fred Adler, a New York attorney, who agreed to a modest investment in a struggling new company known as Data General Corporation. It is rumored that the four principals each made in excess of $10 million within four years of launching this venture.

With these positive examples in mind, complete the questionnaire in Figure 6.1 as background for developing your own business plan.

Figure 6.1 Information Questionnaire

To Be Used as Background for the Development of a Business Plan

1. What is the present name of the company?

2. Is the company a corporation, partnership or sole proprietorship?

3. If the company is a corporation, please set forth the date and the state of incorporation.

4. Furnish the names of the persons who caused the company to be formed.

5. Was the company originally organized as a corporation, partnership or sole proprietorship?

6. Furnish the names of the initial shareholders and/or providers of funds (debt and equity) of the company. Supply dates of each sale of securities, number of shares issued and the consideration received for the shares. If no cash consideration was received, indicate the dollar value ascribed to such consideration.

7. Describe the nature of the company's business. Has the nature of the company's business changed or evolved since its inception? Is it intended to place future emphasis on different areas?

8. Does the company conduct business under names other than its own? If so, please set forth the names and places where they are used.

9. Does the company utilize any trademarks or tradenames? If so, submit copies.

10. What geographical areas does the company serve? Are there any limitations on what markets can be reached, e.g., freight, duties, service, maintenance, patent licenses, tariffs, government regulation, etc.? Does the company intend to enlarge its present areas of distribution or service?

11. Describe the major products or services of the company.

12. In which states or countries other than its state of incorporation is the company licensed or qualified to do business?

13. Furnish a listing plus a physical description of all offices, plants, laboratories, warehouses, stores, outlets, studios or other facilities (include size of plot, square footage of enclosed space, etc.).

14. Describe the method or methods of distribution and sales. If any contractual arrangements are involved, please describe and/or furnish copies.

15. List and describe to the degree relevant, all patents, technical information, trademarks, franchises, copyrights, patent and technical information, licenses owned and/or used.

16. Furnish a detailed five-year breakdown of sales, earnings, income or losses

---

Figure 6.1 continued

---

of the company's major divisions, departments and product categories. Give percentage of total income or loss attributed to each.

17. Furnish a detailed breakdown of major suppliers of raw materials, goods, etc. Give their names, addresses and volume of purchases. Are other sources readily available or is the company dependent to any degree on any one supplier? What would result if the products of said suppliers were no longer readily procurable? Does the company have any long-term contracts with its suppliers?

18. If the company utilizes the services of subcontractors or processors of its products or components of subassemblies, describe the work done and the availability of other subcontractors or processors. Does the company have any long-term contracts with such persons?

19. Furnish a three-year record of names, addresses and volume of purchases of major customers or outlets for the company's products or services. The prospectus or offering circular will list names of customers who account for more than 10 percent of the company's business. Could this in any way be deleterious to the company?

20. Furnish names of the company's major competitors; describe the nature and area of their competition—is it direct or indirect? What is the company's approximate rank in the industry? Are there numerous competitors? What is the degree of competition? Can new companies readily enter the field? Do the company's competitors possess greater financial resources? Are they longer established and better recognized?

21. List all officers or directors, along with the following data:
    - age
    - education
    - title and function (responsibilities)
    - length of service with company
    - posts held and functions performed for company prior to present post
    - compensation
    - past business associations and posts held
    - special distinctions
    - other directorates or present business affiliations

22. Furnish a copy of all stock option plans.

23. Furnish a copy of or describe any bonus and profit sharing plans.

24. Furnish copies of or describe any other employee fringe benefits.

25. Furnish copies of any pension plans.

26. State the total number of employees, full and part time, the major categories of employees and members within each. If the company is to any degree dependent on technology or other expertise, please give details (e.g., number of PhDs, MAs, engineers, technicians, medical personnel, etc.).

27. Are your employees represented by one or more unions? List each union by name or number. Furnish copies of the union contracts.

28. Furnish a general description of labor relations, past strikes, handling of grievances, etc. Has the company experienced any difficulties in obtaining qualified personnel? Has the company had any problems with respect to personnel turnover?

29. Describe all acquisitions of other companies, assets, personnel, etc., made by the company, or any intended acquisitions. Furnish copies of all acquisition agreements.

30. Describe any major dispositions of subsidiaries, divisions, assets, equipment, plants, etc., made by the company.

31. Has any officer, director or major shareholder ever: (a) had any difficulties of any nature with the Securities and Exchange Commission, the National Association of Securities Dealers or any state securities commission or agency? (b) been convicted of a felony? (c) been under indictment, investigation or threatened by the SEC, NASD, a state commission, or public agency with prosecution for violation of a state or federal statute? Has any such person ever been adjudicated as bankrupt? If the answer to any of the questions is yes, describe the circumstances in detail.

32. Has the company made any private placements of its equity or debt securities or any public sale of its equity or debt securities? If so, furnish complete details, including copies of documents used in the placement or sale.

33. Furnish a specimen copy of all outstanding and authorized equity and debt securities.

34. Furnish the following data regarding the distribution of the company's voting stock:
    - classes of stock and number of shares of each outstanding
    - total number of shareholders plus list of shareholders
    - names, residence addresses and shareholdings of ten largest shareholders of each class
    - relationships of major shareholders to each other or to the officers and directors of the company
    - details of any voting trust agreements, shareholder agreements or other arrangements to vote stock jointly

---

Figure 6.1   continued

---

35. Are there any options to purchase stock or other securities or warrants outstanding other than employee stock option plans? If so, furnish copies or describe such plans.

36. Does the company have any long-term or short-term debt, secured or unsecured, or has the company guaranteed such debt on behalf of others? Furnish copies of the documents creating the debt or guarantee, or describe the debt or guarantee.

37. Furnish detailed audited statements for the last five years if available.

38. Furnish interim statements covering the period subsequent to the last audited financial statement.

39. Furnish comparative figures of earning and net worth for five years.

40. Furnish an explanation of any and all abnormal, nonrecurring or unusual items in earnings statements or balance sheets.

41. Furnish a statement of cash flow if materially different from statement of net earnings.

42. Furnish a statement as to any contingent or possible liabilities not shown on balance sheet. Include guarantees, warranties, litigation, etc.

43. With respect to the company's inventories, state major categories, method used in valuation (LIFO, FIFO, other) and control systems. If your inventories are distinctive in any fashion (e.g., film libraries, promotional displays, etc.), state how they are handled on your books.

44. What is the company's policy regarding depreciation, depletion and amortization? Which items are capitalized and which expensed? Are there any deferred write-offs?

45. Are your company's methods of accounting similar to those used in the rest of the industry? If not, please describe the differences and the reason for such differences.

46. Describe the status of federal and state tax examinations. When was your last examination, and are there any open questions?

47. Describe all bank relationships and credit lines. Are factors involved?

48. Describe any pending or threatened claims and litigation. Identify the parties, the amounts involved, the names of persons involved and furnish copies of all documents with respect thereto.

49. Describe all insurance coverages (e.g., plant, equipment, properties, work interruption, key employees).

50. Describe your company's projection of sales and earnings for the next three years, including explanations with respect to any increase or decrease.

51. List all real estate owned by the company, including, without limitation, the following: (a) the improvements on the property, (b) the assessed valuation and amount of current real estate taxes, (c) any mortgages, including amounts, rates of interest and due dates, (d) any liens or encumbrances and (e) the estimated present value.

52. List all real estate leased by the company, including, without limitation, the following: (a) the amount of space, (b) the rent-fixed and contingent, (c) the term of lease, (d) the renewal options, (e) the purchase options, (f) the minimum annual gross rentals and (g) the minimum total gross rental obligation to expiration of all leases in force.

53. List all equipment leased by the company if aggregate annual rentals exceed $5,000 or if the company is dependent on the equipment. If any other property is leased at a sizeable aggregate annual rental, please furnish details of the lease, including without limitation the terms, options to renew and/or purchase, etc.

54. Describe all depreciable property owned by the company including, without limitation, the following: (a) the original cost to the company, (b) the depreciation to date, in addition to a statement as to the method employed, (c) the remaining cost and (d) the aging of items listed (remaining depreciable life).

55. Furnish copies of all brochures, catalogues, mailers, publicity releases, newspaper or magazine articles, literature and the like distributed by the company or concerning the company, its products, personnel or services.

56. Describe the company's research and development activities.

57. Describe any unusual contracts relating to the company, its business, products or services.

58. Describe exactly how the net proceeds (after underwriting commission and all expenses) are to be used by the company.

59. Describe the company's plans for expansion or growth.

60. Set forth any information not previously disclosed in your answers that an investor would use in deciding whether to invest in the company.

61. Furnish copies of the following:
    - certificate of incorporation and all amendments
    - bylaws and all amendments
    - employment agreements, if any

■ Typical Table of Contents for a Business Plan

I. History
II. Business Summary

III.   Manufacturing Plan
IV.   Production and Personnel Plan
V.   Products or Services
VI.   Marketing and Sales
VII.   Competition
VIII.   Research and Development
IX.   Management
X.   Financial Reports Supplied by the Company and Explanations
XI.   Capitalization or Equity Structure
XII.   Capitalization or Debt Structure

I.   History of the Company
    A. Indicate date and place of incorporation as well as preincorporation organizational structure.
    B. List founding shareholders and directors.
    C. Describe important changes in the structure of company, its management or its ownership. Set forth predecessor companies, subsidiaries and divisions in an easy-to-understand manner.
    D. Describe company's major successes or achievements to date.

II.   Business Summary
    A. List principal products or services.
    B. Describe the unique features of the business and the products. Compare these objectively with the competition. Give specific goals on annual sales growth and profits and relate to actual past performance.
    C. Give a detailed breakdown of sales or services for the current year and for the past five years. Indicate the cost of goods sold and the pretax profit by product line for all products or services that contribute more than 10 percent in pretax profits.
    D. Break down sales by industries, including U.S. (military versus nonmilitary) and export.
    E. List product brand names, price range and quality.
    F. Capital goods versus consumer goods. How cyclical or seasonal?
    G. Describe patents, trademarks and other trade advantages such as geographic or labor advantages. List expiration dates, if any, and impact on sales, profits and marketing strategy.
    H. Give the statistical record of the industry or subindustry in which the company operates, with an evaluation of its prospects.
    I. Discuss the problems of technological obsolescence, product life and competition.

J. Describe any technological trends or potentialities within the business environment that might be favorable or unfavorable to the company.

III. Manufacturing Plan
   A. Fill in:
      1. plant location
      2. square feet
      3. number of floors
      4. type of construction age
      5. acres of land
      6. owned or leased and value
      7. lease expiration
      8. annual rent
   B. Describe levels of current operations. Estimate the capacity and the current percentage utilization of plan and equipment.
   C. List auto equipment, including delivery trucks, number of vehicles and whether rented or owned. What are the lease arrangements?
   D. Describe the company's depreciation policies. How does it account for the wear on its assets? Over what time period and at what rate are these assets being depreciated?
   E. What manufacturing or office equipment is leased?
   F. Describe plant equipment (enclose evaluation if possible):
      1. major equipment
      2. condition
      3. location
      4. owned or leased and value (estimate)
   G. Describe the plan layout. Is it efficient?
   H. What is the general housekeeping condition?
   I. Is the operation job-shop or mass-production oriented? Does it build custom products per individual jobs, or is it a mass-produced product that can be manufactured under cost-efficient methods and inventoried?
   J. Incremental increase in space and equipment required for $1,000,000 increase in sales. For each major increment of expansion in revenue, is an equal, more or less increment necessary in facilities, people and equipment?
   K. Explain the logic of the plant location(s).
   L. What future capital expenditures for plant and machinery are planned? How will they be financed?

M. What major capital improvements have been made in the past few years? What was their cost and how were they financed?

N. Are any sales of assets planned? On what basis—cash or deferred payments?

O. How many daily shifts are worked. Percentage of overtime. Breakdown by departments. Economics of a two-shift or three-shift schedule.

IV. Production and Personnel Plan

A. Briefly describe your manufacturing operation.

B. List number of personnel and break down by function.

C. Indicate union affiliation and strike history.

D. Describe turnover and morale.

E. Describe labor market (description of important skills) and competition for labor.

F. Calculate percent of labor content in cost of goods sold by product.

G. Describe fringe benefits provided and cost percentage to wages.

H. Does the company rate itself as a low-cost, high-cost or average-cost employer? What is the unemployment rate based upon the business's past hiring and firing practices charged to the company by the state government?

I. What steps are being taken to improve production methods.

J. Are competent people assigned to production planning?

K. Describe quality control procedures.

L. Unit costs versus production levels, detailing fixed and variable costs.

V. Products or Services

A. List principal suppliers, location, product volume, officers dealt with.

B. Briefly describe significant materials and supplies, including availability. Are the storage and material handling facilities adequate?

C. Are purchase economies available? Are purchase discounts available?

D. Are make-or-buy decisions made?

E. What is the average inventory turnover within the company's industry? Explain any deviations for your firm.

F. Does the finished inventory have a shelf-life?

G. Methods of inventory valuation.

H. Current inventory status of distributors and ultimate users.

VI. Marketing and Sales
   A. Describe the market. History, size, trend and your product's position in the market. Identify source of estimates and assumptions.
   B. Is the market at the take-off stage? Project the market back five years and forward five years.
   C. Where are the products sold, and who is the essential end user?
   D. Are the products sold by salaried or commissioned sales force, by distributors or by brokers?
   E. Are accounts receivable sold, discounted or pledged? If so, to whom, at what discount, with or without recourse? If receivables are pledged to a loaning source, either the lender or the borrower actually receives the cash. If they are discounted, the lender gives a percentage of the receivables at the moment they are pledged as collateral. Recourse means that the lender can recover any bad debt on an uncollectible receivable from the borrower, thus lowering the lender's risk.
   F. Number of customers or active accounts and the amount of accounts receivable due over 90 days.
   G. How many customers make up 80 percent of the sales?
      1. principal customers
      2. location
      3. product
      4. volume
      5. percent of company's sales
      6. officer dealt with
   H. Describe any special relationships with customers.
   I. Describe pricing policies with respect to all product lines. How sensitive are prices to costs?
   J. Indicate current backlog and current shippable backlog. The shippable backlog can be shipped and billed immediately upon completing the manufacturing of the product.
   K. How many purchase orders are on hand at present (dollar amount)?
   L. Enclose copies of warranties on present products.
   M. Enclose copies of advertising plan and budget.
   N. Is business seasonal? If so, explain peaks in production, sales, etc.
   O. Calculate selling costs as a percentage of revenues. How will these vary with more or less sales volume?
   P. Explain the customer's primary motivation in purchasing your product: price, delivery time, performance, etc.
   Q. Are any proposed government regulations expected to affect your market?

VII.   Competition
    A.   List major competitors and locations.
       1.   sales
       2.   earnings
       3.   percent of market
       4.   strengths and weaknesses
    B.   Nature of competition: cut-throat or permissive; poorly or well financed.
    C.   Evaluate your competitive advantages and disadvantages. Be specific.
    D.   Is new competition entering the field?
    E.   Compare your company's prices with those of the competition.
    F.   Calculate what share of the business you receive by market area.
    G.   Describe service arrangements and service experience.
    H.   Describe advertising and promotional efforts. Discuss the importance of brand names and trademarks.
    I.   List any independent firms, publications or outside agencies that have evaluated your firm against competitors.
    J.   Explain effects of regulatory agencies, including government.

VIII. Research and Development
    A.   Amount or percent of sales spent per annum in the past five years and projected. Compare with competitors. Detail any capitalized R & D costs.
    B.   Number of employees in this area. Advanced college degrees.
    C.   Detail product developments and R & D that is not related to specific products or services, which is basically research and not development.
    D.   Percent of current sales generated by past R & D.
    E.   State any new field your firm contemplates entering: Is it complementary to the present product or service line?
    F.   List any outside consulting R & D relationships such as firms, universities and individuals. State the percentage of total R & D budget let to outside sources.
    G.   Funding and its consistency from government sources.

IX.   Management
    A.   Develop an organization chart.
    B.   Include resumes and references.
    C.   Complete credit and personal investigation checks.
    D.   Analyze management's reputation, capabilities and attitude (analysis of team: one-man show, executive turnover, morale).

    E. Profit consciousness: Is there an on-going profit improvement plan? An executive incentive program?

    F. Analyze the company's innovative ability. How is creativity fostered?

    G. Provide a schedule of past, current and proposed salaries and other compensation for each member of management or owners, including bonuses, fee arrangements and profit sharing. List key personnel along with annual salaries, bonuses and fees.

    H. If a stock option or other management incentive plan is in effect, provide an outline.

    I. How are salary increases for management controlled?

    J. List directors other than officers and employees (name, title, compensation, shares of stock owned, common and preferred stock).

    K. Does the company carry life insurance on its officers (amount and company)?

    L. Enclose any contract or proposed contract between the firm and any member of management, any stockholder or any outside consultant.

X.   Financial Reports Supplied by the Company and Explanations

    A. Provide audited annual reports for the past five years, including balance sheets, profit and loss statements, and statements of sources and applications of funds.

    B. Provide current financial reports, with officers' statements as to material changes in condition.

    C. Provide pro forma balance sheets giving the effect of the proposed financing on a quarterly basis for two years.

    D. Develop month-by-month projections of profit and loss, cash receipts and disbursements for the two-year period.

    E. Develop yearly projections of revenues and earnings for five years.

    F. Analyze sales by markets, products and profits.

    G. Record of the industry or subindustry in which the company operates to contrast with the performance of the specific business.

XI.   Capitalization: Equity

    A. Total shares authorized: common _____ preferred _____.

    B. Total shares outstanding: common _____ preferred _____.

    C. Describe principal terms, including voting rights, dividend payments and conversion features for each class of stock.

    D. If a private company, list all shareholders. If a public company, list all shareholders who directly or indirectly control more than 5 percent of the outstanding voting stock.

E. If any of the shareholders are not members of the company's management, describe their motivation for becoming shareholders.

F. If individuals or entities who might be considered founders, promoters or insiders under any law are no longer shareholders, describe the reason for their withdrawal from the business.

G. Provide a chronological list of sales of stock, stating prices, terms, number of buyers and their names.

H. Describe any other transactions involving the principal shareholders and the company (e.g., real estate, equipment leases or sales, loans to or from shareholders, voting trusts).

I. Describe accounting principles regarding depreciation, R&D, taxes, inventories and so forth.

J. Are the tax returns of the company and its subsidiaries for the past five years included?

K. If the business is seasonal, explain its cycle and relate it to the company's financial needs.

L. Discuss the aging of accounts receivable and accounts payable.

M. List the losses from bad debts over the past five years.

N. Describe the trend and give percentages for the following:
    1. sales and increases or decreases
    2. cost of goods sold
    3. overhead, fixed and variable
    4. selling expenses
    5. research and development
    6. taxes
    7. pretax and after-tax profit margins
    8. return on total capital, including long-term debt
    9. return on total equity
    10. industry trends in each of the above areas

O. Does the balance sheet contain hidden or undervalued assets or liabilities?

P. Discuss any nonrecurring items of income or expense in recent financial statements.

Q. Describe the company's profit improvement plan.

R. What years' tax returns have been audited?

S. Are all taxes paid?

T. Are there any disputes between the company and any taxing authority?

XII. Capitalization: Debt
    A. Principal bank; name of officer handling account.
    B. List the following for each long-term debt obligation:

      1. lender and contact officer
      2. total amount
      3. initial date
      4. length of term
      5. sinking fund
      6. date of maturity
      7. security or collateral

C. Are seasonal bank loans required? What was the largest amount borrowed in each of the past two years? Minimum?

D. List the amounts of current lines of credit, and with whom.

E. Describe all contingent liabilities.

F. Debt-to-equity ratio: for company _____ ; for industry _____ .

G. What guarantees are currently required by lenders?

■ A Good Plan Is Not Enough

A "good" business plan is one that raises money; a "bad" plan does not attract investors. But the entrepreneur must remember that a good plan and a good business are not necessarily synonymous. A good plan may raise money, but the business may still fail. However, a bad plan almost always means business failure. In order to succeed in reaching the more crucial objectives of a profitable business, a good plan plus a good business is required.

The five-minute process is so cold in concept that it may alienate many businesspeople. The business becomes part of life and the plan becomes the essence of the business. Hence, to add a degree of warmth and a bit more understanding to the central aspect of small business, actual business plans should be interpreted against the process outlined in this chapter.

While dealing in this abstract area, remember a quotation that links entrepreneurs and venture capitalists: *The men who manage men manage the men who manage things,* but *the men who manage money manage the men who manage men.*

Here's a graphic representation of that thought:

Pecking Order	Ease of Handling	
	Venture Capitalist	Entrepreneur
1. Money	High	Low
2. Men	Medium	Medium
3. Things	Low	High

■ ■

7

How To Get a Business Loan Without Signing Your Life Away

One of the greatest differences between entrepreneurs and corporate executives is that entrepreneurs have to be able to deal with banks and bankers. It's not easy, and it's not fun, but it is a critical transition from being a mid-career executive to being a business owner.

The purpose of this chapter is to make you the best customer your banker ever had. That means not only getting a business loan, but selecting a bank, developing a relationship with your banker, knowing how to negotiate a loan and avoiding personal loan guarantees. But before I give you any advice on the subject of getting a business loan, you must complete the Banker's Quiz in Figure 7.1. In Chapter 2 I gave you the Entrepreneur's Quiz and in Chapter 4 the Franchise Quiz. The Banker's Quiz is different because it is not about you, but about your banker.

Figure 7.1   The Banker's Quiz

Circle yes or no. Then compare your score with that of the 310 members of the CEO Club who scored an average of 175 points out of a possible 330.

1. Can you draw an organization chart of the bank showing your banker's position?

   Yes   No   25 points

2. Did you give your banker a small (under $25) Christmas or other holiday gift last year?

   Yes   No   20 points

3. Do you know where your banker went to school?

   Yes   No   10 points

4. Do you know your banker's spouse's first name?

   Yes   No   10 points

5. Do you know your banker's boss's first and last name?

   Yes   No   15 points

6. Can you give the names and backgrounds of at least two other members of the loan committee? (20 points each)

   Yes   No   40 points

7. Do you know your banker's hometown?

   Yes   No   10 points

8. Do you know your banker's birthday?

   Yes   No   15 points

9. Have you taken your banker or his or her boss on a tour of your facilities in the last six months?

   Yes   No   25 points

10. Have you gone out socially with your banker and his or her spouse (not as part of a loan request) in the last six months?

    Yes   No   30 points

11. Did you refer a good customer (depositor) to the bank in the last year?

    Yes   No   50 points

12. Did you send your banker's secretary one red rose on Secretary's Day last year?

    Yes   No   20 points

13. Did you sign your banker's name to the gift instead of yours?

    Yes   No   20 points

14. Did you invite your banker to your Christmas party or company picnic last year?

    Yes   No   20 points

15. Does your banker know your lawyer and accountant on a first-name basis? (10 points each)

    Yes   No   20 points

■ Scoring on the Banker's Quiz

The correct answer to every question is yes. To be your bank's best customer, you need to score 200 points or better on this quiz. Here's why:

1. Today, so much of banking is branch banking that you need to know where the decision-making power is and where your banker fits into it.

2. When I say small gift, I mean something like a book. If you know your banker has a hobby, such as boating, give him or her a book on the subject. It shows that you think of the person as a human being, not merely a banker.

3. One of the first things two people do when they get to know each other is to look for some common ground. Knowing what school your banker went to will not only tell you something about him, it can often provide an opener like "We played you in football," or "My brother did his undergraduate work there."

4. Again, people tend to trust familiarity, so it helps if you know your banker's spouse's name, and ask after him or her once in a while.

5. It's the nature of the banking business that bankers tend to move up quickly in their jobs—either changing banks or bouncing from one branch to another. If you know your banker's boss (and he or she knows you), then it's possible that when your banker moves, your account will be passed up to the boss rather than down to the new loan officer. And the higher the person you're dealing with, the better off you are.

6. Ninety percent of the time, your loan officer will make the decision on your loan, but it still has to be approved by the loan committee. If you know who's on the committee (and they know you), that will expedite the process.

7. Again, familiarity and common ground are the keys to a good relationship. The more you know about your banker, the easier it is to strengthen and develop those ties.

8. Whenever I mention that it's a good idea to give your banker a quick phone call on his birthday, people laugh and tell me that's just a little too corny. They laugh, that is, 364 days a year, but on *their* birthday they get a kick out of the fact that someone remembers. (Also, calling your banker on his birthday suggests that you have a good memory for dates and will remember the date your loan payments come due.)

9. A banker has an amazing change in attitude when he or she actually sees a product being produced, sold and shipped. If you're in a service business, like real estate, more important than showing your banker your office is driving past houses you've sold or ones you currently have listed.

10. When I say you should take your banker out socially (to dinner, for instance), I mean socially. No business. And don't make the mistake of asking a touchy question after a pleasant meal. (Something like, "My wife is a little worried about the fact that you want her signature on a loan, and she thinks it would be a good idea to discuss it with you while your wife is here" is a definite no-no.) And let your banker do 90 percent of the talking. The more you let him talk about his interests, the better impression you'll make.

I could continue with the answers to questions 11–15, but seasoned executives can figure them out for themselves. A little help is okay, but too much is not helpful. It reminds me of what one mid-career executive told me over a few beers: "Joe, I really appreciated all the help you gave me, and the good news is that I received the loan. The bad news is that I can't pay it back!"

So, I only prime the pump.

■ How to Avoid Personal Loan Guarantees

Think of banking negotiations as a pyramid. The tip is the personal loan guarantee. This issue is so critical that I've written a whole book on the subject—*How to Get a Business Loan Without Signing Your Life Away* (Simon & Schuster, 1992).

Bankers are generally orderly people; they prefer a two-step process—first the loan, then the guarantee. After the loan is negotiated, they like to say, "By the way, with all business loans we require the borrower to fill out a personal financial statement." Your objective is a one-step negotiation with the guarantee worked out as part of the loan application. Your ultimate goal is to have the guarantee waived altogether.

Following is my 12-point approach for staying off personal loan guarantees.

1. Watch what you sign—and how you sign it.
2. Decide what it's worth.
3. Protect your home—offer other collateral.
4. Find out if everyone has to guarantee a loan.
5. Never let a spouse who doesn't work with you be forced to cosign.
6. Ask for money when you don't need it.
7. Pay attention to the form of the guarantee.
8. Use multiple stockholders to limit your liability.
9. Have your board of directors sign a policy statement against personal guarantees.
10. Build your case piece by piece.
11. Don't get on in the first place.
12. Help your banker be a hero.

Watch What You Sign

Your signature is not an autograph. As an officer of a business, you must be careful about what documents you sign and how you sign them. It can be a painful lesson. Consider the case of an officer for a Florida real estate company. In 1986, the firm entered into a loan agreement with a bank. The company officer signed a contract stating that the firm would repay the credit extension plus interest.

When the company defaulted, the officer was billed nearly $200,000 for the debt, the interest and the attorney's fee. He argued that it was a corporate debt, not a personal liability, but a federal court in Florida ruled against him. Why? Because the man did not include his official title when he signed his name. According to Florida law, the signature of a company's agent leaves the signor personally liable for meeting the terms of the contract unless there is some evidence that the signing was made in a representative capacity (e.g., as president).

Decide What It's Worth

This step is crucial because it will prevent the banker from taking advantage of your emotional desire to get off the personal loan guarantee. Set limits for yourself before negotiations begin, keeping in mind the following considerations:

■ *Interest rates.* Would you pay a higher rate if you didn't have to sign personally for the loan?

■ *Amount of money.* Would you be willing to borrow less in exchange for not having to sign a personal guarantee?

■ *Maturity.* Would you settle for a shorter maturity on your loan?

■ *Compensating balance.* Would you be willing to put up a higher compensating balance for the money you've borrowed?

Of these four considerations, a higher compensating balance might seem to be the most painless offer to make for release from a personal loan guarantee. After all, you have to keep your cash somewhere—why not keep it at the bank in the form of a compensating balance? Your banker will encourage you to do this. Bankers like compensating balances because, as a rule, banks have a capital base of only 5 percent. This means they can take your compensating balance of, say, $150 and potentially turn it into $3,000 in interest-earning loans. You're probably thinking: Compensating balances won't cost me anything. After all, I've got to keep some cash at the bank anyway, and it'll make my banker happy.

This reasoning is problematic because it overlooks the fact that compensating balances raise the actual rate of interest on your loan. It works like this: You borrow $1,000 from the bank at 12 percent interest, but you are asked to leave $150 in the bank as a compensating balance. This seems relatively painless because it leaves you with $850 to use. Your actual rate of interest now, though, is not 12 percent. It is 12 percent divided by 0.85, or 14.1 percent. If you are not willing to pay that rate of interest, do not agree to leave that compensating balance. If 14 percent is a better interest rate than the banker is willing to offer if you don't leave a compensating balance then, of course, you'll want to reconsider.

Compensating balances and idle balances are part of cash management, a subject too large for this book. You should, however, be aware of a study by the Caruth Institute of Owner-Managed Business at Southern Methodist University in Dallas, Texas. The study showed that a major bank's pretax earnings on small business loans were 2.7 percentage points higher than its earnings on loans to large firms, in spite of the higher administrative costs and greater risks of small business loans. The small businesses were paying an average of 17.7 percent interest instead of the 15.0 percent interest averaged by large businesses.

The reason for this, the study revealed, was that small businesses didn't manage their idle cash as well as large firms. They left more of their funds in idle cash balances than the bank could lend. If your financial officer and accountant are not well versed in cash management, you may have a weak catcher and center fielder.

Protect Your Home—Offer Other Collateral

I have long argued the unfairness of the banking and legal system that currently requires small business owners to "bet the homestead" on every decision. The same has never been required of officers of larger businesses even though bank and big business failures have become almost as common as small business failures.

Try offering a piece of collateral as a means of staying off a personal loan guarantee. If you have a second home, offer it as collateral. As assignment on a second home is better than a personal blanket guarantee on everything you own. By doing this, you protect your primary homestead.

Homesteading is another way of protecting your home. In the last century, many states enacted legislation stating that a lender who lent you money for an asset other than your primary residence could not take your principal residence toward payment on the loan. In simple language, it meant that if a farmer bought a tractor and stopped making payments on it, the lender couldn't confiscate the farm. The farmer could file a piece of paper called the Homestead Act to protect his principal residence.

The Homestead Act still exists in more than half the states, and many lawyers recommend that you take advantage of it. Depending on the state, you file one piece of paper with the registrar of deeds in your town, and it protects a certain amount of equity in the home. (In some states, homesteading is automatic and you don't need to file anything.) In Massachusetts, for example, homesteading protects $40,000 of the equity in your home. If your home is worth $100,000 and a secondary lender (not the bank that has the mortgage on your home) tries to take your home to pay a debt on which you've defaulted, he has to leave $40,000 of equity in the home. In Florida, Texas and Oklahoma, you can protect the entire homestead and all its equity.

The fact that you've filed the Homestead Act paperwork on your home might not show up when you fill out the loan application or the personal financial information unless the bank decides to do a title search, which is rarely done unless you are specifically pledging your home as collateral. Ask your lawyer whether your home qualifies for homesteading, and be sure you're up to date on changes in state laws.

A recent decision by bankruptcy Judge Marvin A. Holland, in Brooklyn,

New York, could have far-reaching implications for personal loan guarantees. The judge rejected as unconstitutional a law requiring a person in bankruptcy to sell the couple's home to satisfy creditors.

Bernard and Stuart Persky are a father and son team whose restaurant borrowed $120,000 from the bank, which they personally guaranteed. The chief assets of each were separate homes in Staten Island valued by the court papers at $129,000 each. In his 68-page ruling, Judge Holland wrote that a provision of the 1978 federal bankruptcy code allowing courts to force the sale of homes was unconstitutional because it affects the spouse, who is not a debtor. In addition, he held that trustees couldn't force the sale of a home under the state's power to take property to help a creditor recover "public interest." The case would have value as a precedent only if homes are jointly held by the couple. The provision of the bankruptcy code, Judge Holland added, "interferes with property rights held by a third party, a noncreditor-stranger to the bankruptcy proceedings, just because that third party's rights may affect the value of the debtor's property rights."

The case may be appealed by Community National Bank, which has been taken over by the Federal Deposit Insurance Corporation (FDIC). But if the decision stands, the protection offered in entrepreneurial states such as Florida, Texas and Oklahoma could be provided nationwide.

Find Out If Everyone Has to Guarantee a Loan

If your banker says everyone has to sign personally for corporate debt, find out how big you have to be to avoid signing. You want to know where your bank draws the line. Also, seek out small business owners who are borrowing without personal guarantees. Determine what they have that you don't.

Don't hesitate to mention Lee Iacocca. Try this approach:

When Chrysler found itself in trouble and borrowed all that money, Lee Iacocca didn't have to sign a personal guarantee for the money did he? Did any members of Chrysler's team have to guarantee the debt? Why should I? I'm not borrowing as much as they did, and my company is in better shape than Chrysler was at the time. Iacocca was a lot less likely to turn Chrysler around than I am to keep my profitable business profitable. Why should I have to guarantee a small loan on a solid company?

Don't be afraid to get indignant:

It's not fair! Banks discriminate against little guys like me and let big fish like Iacocca off the hook. You're discriminating against the backbone of the U.S. economy—the entrepreneur—and if you don't believe me, just think of all the small farmers in the Midwest who are being victimized by your double standard.

Your banker will probably say, "But Chrysler is a public company, so it's not controlled by its officers."
Here's a comeback:

Did you know that Iacocca's salary for the year Chrysler received that debt package was one dollar? And his salary for the year he saved the business was $20.6 million. That sure sounds like an entrepreneurial company to me.

Never Let a Spouse Who Doesn't Work with You Cosign Your Loan

If your spouse does not work with you in the business, don't let him or her cosign your loan. It used to be common procedure for a businessman to take his loan agreement home to his wife for her to sign somewhere between cooking dinner and putting the kids to bed. Nowadays, though, husbands are being asked to cosign loan agreements even more than wives. In either case, the days of automatic signing of a personal loan guarantee by a spouse are over because in today's two-income households many spouses have their own assets to protect. Pressuring your spouse to sign the guarantee can destroy a relationship.

If your banker asks for your spouse's signature, make it tough. Say:

I understand your policy is to have my wife sign, but Mary doesn't understand the necessity of this. She wants to talk to you herself. I'm sorry, but I really have little choice in the matter, so you're going to have to talk to her yourself about signing. Frankly, I don't see how the bank can be so chauvinistic as to require my spouse to do this. After all, she is just an innocent third party.

Let your spouse defend himself or herself. Spouses usually make a pretty strong case for not being part of the personal guarantee. (You can always tell your spouse to say: "Did Lee Iacocca's wife have to cosign his loan for Chrysler?") Ask your lawyer about recent court cases concerning the liabilities of innocent spouses; they are being decided increasingly in favor of the spouse.

Ask for Money When You Don't Need It

Considering I'm talking about timing, I'd like to introduce Mancuso's Law: *The only time to raise capital is when you don't need it.*

Banks prefer to lend money to borrowers who have borrowed at least once and have paid back at least one loan on time. It's a psychological factor, just as they prefer to lend to a business that already has an account at the bank. Take advantage of your banker's methodical nature. Bankers remember everything; they're like elephants with file cabinets instead of trunks.

Bankers like to hear from you frequently; it makes them feel more secure about their loan to you. I recommend monthly payments on a loan over payment every six months. Keep your banker up to date on your business.

If you're going to request a new loan in six months, mention to your banker *now* that you are working on an exciting expansion that might require more credit. When you actually make your request three months later, it will confirm your reliability. Otherwise, if you walk in saying you're out of money and need more for expansion, the banker will treat what is basically an identical request with suspicion and mistrust.

Remember to invite your banker to your facilities to see the results of your latest loan. Bankers love an excuse to get out of their offices, and they need to understand your business and see it in operation to be totally comfortable about lending you money.

Pay Attention To the Form of the Guarantee

There are two basic types of guarantees: *joint and several* and *payment versus collection* (indemnity versus guarantee). Are you guaranteeing the payment of the debt or the collection of the debt? In other words, if the business fails, can the bank sue you and the business simultaneously and proceed against both entities aggressively until it gets paid (joint and several guarantee), or does it have to sue the business first and, if it fails to get the money from the business, then go after you (payment versus collection guarantee)?

The bank would prefer the joint and several guarantee—it would rather sue you and the company simultaneously than have to wait until it finds out it can't get the money from the company to go after you. This is a negotiating point. If you can get an indemnification guarantee instead of a joint and several guarantee, you are one step closer to establishing yourself as a customer who does not sign personal guarantees. Just knowing that there are different kinds of guarantees will help you to negotiate. For example, you could give up your push for an indemnification guarantee late in the negotiations and ask your banker to give up something in return.

Still another aspect of the guarantee is when it goes into effect. Tell your banker you don't want to sign the personal guarantee, but arrange a scenario that will trigger when the guarantee will go into effect; in this way, you are not guaranteeing the debt unless certain unlikely events occur. Here are a few conditions:

- You miss three consecutive loan payments.

- Working capital falls below a specified amount.

- Net worth falls below a specified amount.

One more thing: Avoid the entrepreneur's innate tendency to act like a blowfish when it comes to filling out the personal financial statement required by the bank. Do not exaggerate the value of assets; this tactic will only come back to haunt you. The best bet is not to inflate your net worth, but show the truth (or a little less than the truth). Keep in mind that the personal loan guarantee and the personal financial statement act as a directory for the bank's lawyer to find where you keep attachable assets (typically real estate) in case your company defaults on the loan.

These are legal points. I advise you to consult with your lawyer continuously during the negotiations, but don't let your lawyer negotiate for you. Do it yourself.

Use Multiple Stockholders To Limit Your Liability

There is a second negotiating point concerning the form of the guarantee. If your company has multiple stockholders, you can negotiate for limited guarantees. Try to share the personal guarantee liability with the other major stockholders of your company. For example, if you have five equal stockholders, the bank will seek to have each of you sign for 100 percent of the loan. During negotiations, ask your banker if each of you can sign for 20 percent of the loan, for a total guarantee of 100 percent.

I handled a negotiation like this for a surveying and mapping company in Massachusetts. The company had five major stockholders, and the bank wanted a 100 percent personal guarantee on a $100,000 loan from each stockholder. Technically, the bank could collect $500,000 on a $100,000 loan by having each partner sign. If you and your four partners sign and the loan goes bad, the bank may decide to go after you because you've got the most assets or the deepest pockets. (People with deep pockets usually have short arms.) You'll then have to sue your partners to have them take responsibility for their share of the loan. It could turn into a long legal mess, and it's not some remote possibility—it happens all the time.

When I went into negotiations for the Massachusetts company, I asked that the personal guarantee be split five ways so that each stockholder was responsible for $20,000. The bank didn't want to do it because it's much more expensive to sue five people for $20,000 each than it is to sue one person for

$100,000. Depending on how the loan guarantee is written, there is often a jury trial, and in most states today it takes about six years just to get a jury trial. Also, the contract statute of limitations is usually for six years. Know the facts in your state about personal loan guarantees before you start negotiations. Ask your lawyer to brief you so you can negotiate intelligently. State laws vary, and you really need good legal advice (and remember, I'm not a lawyer).

Although I didn't come out of the negotiations with a 20 percent guarantee for each stockholder, I did get 50 percent. That's still quite an improvement over 100 percent. Don't be afraid to negotiate. The bank wants to lend you the money and you need the money—both parties ought to be able to find some middle ground on all the issues. In the case of the Massachusetts company, the bank was happy. It had a $250,000 guarantee. The stockholders would have been happier with only 20 percent liability, but they were pleased to have gotten their guarantees halved. In other words, they each guaranteed half of the $100,000 loan or $50,000.

Have Your Board of Directors Sign a Policy Statement Against Personal Guarantees

Early in the history of your business ask your board of directors to vote on this resolution: "Officers and shareholders of this corporation will not be allowed to sign personally for any debt. Any debt for which they sign personally will not be honored by this corporation." Have this resolution signed, dated, notarized and put in your minutes book. Renew it by voting on it at every annual meeting.

When your banker asks you to personally guarantee your first loan, you can pull out your minutes book and show what a tremendous hassle it would be to go to the board of directors and change company policy.

One of our CEO Club members, Dr. Charles Feldman of Cardio-Data in Sudbury, Massachusetts, heard me give this advice ten years ago. He was buying a large piece of medical equipment for his business and the supplier wanted him to sign a personal loan guarantee. The delivery man waltzed into Charles's office with the personal loan guarantee for him to sign. Charles said, "Gee, when I ordered the machine I didn't know you were going to require a personal loan guarantee. That wasn't even discussed."

"Well, I just can't leave it here," the delivery man said. "This piece of equipment is worth three times your whole company. You have to be responsible for it."

Charles pulled out his minutes book and showed him nine years of annual corporate minutes affirming that no officer of the corporation may sign personal loan guarantees on corporate purchases.

"Do you know what I would have to do to undo this?" Charles said. "I'd have to call a meeting of stockholders. The stockholders will have to elect new directors. I don't know when they're going to do this—it could take nine months! I can't sign that thing. If I do, I could be criminally prosecuted for going against the rules of the board of directors."

Now, just between you and me, that statement in the minutes book would hold up in court for about five seconds, but it is a useful and often convincing negotiating tool. In Charles's case, it worked on the truck driver. Every little "policy" helps.

After you show your minutes book to your loan officer and moan about company policy, ask her if everyone signs personally for loans at her bank. Even if all you do is ask this question, you're ahead. You're showing that you're not stupid.

Build Your Case Piece by Piece

If you do end up having to sign personally for your first loan, don't be discouraged. In the real world, you are part of the 99 percent of CEOs who do sign. At least you got the loan, and now you can put all the strategies you've learned to work on your banker to get off the guarantee you're already on and to avoid signing personally for your next loan.

Set future milestones for getting off. Start chipping away at the guarantee from day one. Find out where and when between zero and 100 percent of repayment your banker will let you off the guarantee. As soon as you take out the guarantee, write a letter letting your banker know the guarantee was not given lightly, and that it bothers you.

It may be a slow and tedious process, and it is even possible that your banker won't let you off until you've paid off nine-tenths of the loan, but remember that you are taking on the enormous task of reprogramming her elephantlike memory. That memory will work in your favor on the next loan, when she remembers that letting you off the personal guarantee did not ruin her career.

Try this approach: "On my $100,000 loan, of which I've paid back $50,000, would it be unreasonable for me to ask if I could be released from the personal loan guarantee when I've paid back $75,000? I know I'll sleep better." If she says no, ask her: "If I came in here after I'd paid off $99,990 of that loan, and I told you that the personal guarantee was still causing me sleepless nights, wouldn't you let me off the guarantee?" Of course she'll say, "I don't see why not," and then you've got something to work with. So, you've put the thought in your banker's mind of the possibility of letting you off the guarantee. *The best way to get off a personal loan guarantee is to ask and to continue to ask and bargain after you have shown some sign of your ability to pay back the loan.*

Don't Get On in the First Place

The best thing you can do for your future is to avoid signing for your loans from the very start. Remember your banker's long, elephantlike memory? No banker has ever said to a customer who has been on personal loan guarantees, "Gee, you're such a good customer of the bank, I don't think we need to bother with these silly guarantees any more." It doesn't matter how diligently you have worked to become your banker's best friend and customer, if you signed a personal loan guarantee in the beginning, she'll expect you to sign them from now on, no matter how successful you become. (In practice, most CEOs get off personal loan guarantees by switching banks. The entrepreneur walks into a new bank across the street and says, "I'll bring my business to your bank—same terms and conditions—but no personal guarantees. What do you say?" According to my research, that's how about half of all guarantees are released in the real world.)

By now your banker will have asked you the big guilt question: "Why don't you want to sign personally—aren't you going to pay back the loan?" Bankers practice this question in front of their mirrors at home. They love how it puts you on the spot. You might want to practice your answer just as much.

One way to throw her a curve is with this answer:

"Of course I'm going to pay it back, Joan. You've seen my business plan, the loan is well accounted for. Besides, I've paid back all my other loans, but this isn't that simple. Life is more complicated than sets of numbers would have us believe. It may not be all that logical, but for me this is a big issue. I lose sleep over it. It's like my wife, Matilda, was saying the other day.

She asked me why we couldn't just pay off the mortgage on our beautiful quarter-million-dollar house on Cape Cod. I explained to her that the 6 percent interest on the mortgage is our least expensive borrowed money and it would be foolish to pay it off. Do you know what she told me? She said, 'I know the numbers and the facts, but I've always wanted to live in a house that was all mine, with no mortgage.'

You know, Joan, I guess I feel the same way about the personal loan guarantee. The loan will be paid back with or without the guarantee, but I'll sure sleep better without it. I'll even perform better at work without the extra worry, and we both want me to perform at my best, don't we? Can you relate to my wife's feeling?

If Matilda doesn't work, give your banker this second, more pragmatic reason:

> With the present turmoil in the banking industry, I am very uneasy about personally guaranteeing corporate debt because that decreases my flexibility. If your bank gets in trouble, as Bank of America, Continental Illinois, or Republic did, the personal guarantee could hinder my flexibility while the regulators are undoing the mess at your bank. My only choice in such a predicament might be to borrow elsewhere. The guarantee could prevent me from being able to keep my business going. I think you'll agree that in these times bank failure is not a remote possibility, and that it's unhealthy for both of us to put a ball and chain around the foot of the one person who could bail out the company if the bank gets in trouble.

Now you can see why you've laid such careful groundwork for a warm, friendly relationship with your banker. You want her to understand how you feel about signing that loan guarantee, not just look at the numbers. When she throws you that hard logical question, you can use it as a launching pad for your own "Matilda" story. Then you can get logical again by telling her that, quite frankly, the worry over the guarantee is adversely affecting your performance.

Help Your Banker Be a Hero

Even if you have no track record of previous loans to show your banker, it's not over. It's far more advantageous to have no track record than a bad track record, and you can make your case stronger with a good story. In fact, a good story can be even better than an average track record.

Your job is to give your banker a neatly bundled, coherent, exciting and picturesque story. Your banker would love to go home to her husband and tell him how she single-handedly saved your wonderful new company and made the world a better place.

Remember, your banker will have to go to the loan committee with your request to be released from the personal loan guarantee. She would much rather go to them with a wonderful story than with just a loan guarantee release request.

Let's say your company is producing a new monitoring device for babies that will eliminate crib deaths. Do you ask the banker for a loan to produce an electronic oscilloscope? No! You tell her how her loan to you will protect the children of the community. Make the banker a hero for lending you the money.

It's your responsibility as an entrepreneur to do that for your banker. Perhaps she'll get that promotion. Don't forget to take her to lunch or to a ball game because she's your company's best friend. You'll have a great time, and eventually the efforts you've put into the relationship will pay off, and the need for your personal loan guarantee will be a thing of the past.

A Lawyer's View

The following is a commentary by Levin & Ginsburg Ltd., one of Chicago's premier legal firms, on the topic of avoiding personal guarantees.*

As a CEO for a privately held business you are often asked to personally guarantee loans for your business. This means if the business is unable to repay the lender, you, the guarantor, must personally pay the loan. By providing a personal guarantee on any obligation incurred by your business, you not only substantially increase your potential liability, but you also put too many of your "eggs in one basket" and thereby jeopardize your family's security. Do not allow failure of the business to result in your personal bankruptcy. What can you, the CEO of a privately held business, do to avoid giving a personal guarantee on a loan needed by the business?

Lenders generally require collateral, such as accounts receivable, inventory and equipment, as security for their loan. Lenders to privately held businesses typically seek a guarantee by the CEO because lenders want to be sure their loans will be protected. The value of your personal guarantee may be as important to the lender as collateral. By requiring your personal guarantee a lender receives both your financial and "emotional" commitment to monitor the business and repay the loan. The implications of the financial commitment are clear, while the consequences of the emotional commitment are less apparent. The knowledge the security of your family's "nest egg" depends on your business's success can delay and actually hinder the effective decision making required from a CEO. As a result, your personal guarantee, with its emotional commitment, may weaken your business and lessen its value, both to the lender and to you. The personal guarantee can produce the opposite of its desired effect. Trying to convince your lender of this result could prove very difficult.

---

*Reprinted by permission of Levin & Ginsburg Ltd. The law firm of Levin & Ginsburg consists of 12 attorneys and 22 support staff. It provides a broad range of legal services to entrepreneurs and other businesses, including the negotiating and documentation of commercial loan transactions. The practice stresses client communications, timely service, planning and risk analysis, and general counsel services.

In demanding your personal guarantee, the lender seeks accountability from the CEO, the person who is in control of what is effectively the lender's collateral. As a CEO, you are in a better position than the lender to evaluate market demand, resale value of inventories, maintenance needs of equipment, and the credit worthiness or general desirability of your customers. You do have control over various aspects of the operation of your business, and may agree to be accountable for those. However, you do not have control over market fluctuations or customer purchasing behaviors. Although you may seek to make prudent, informed business decisions, you cannot be assured that the market and your customers will remain stable and unchanged.

Attempt a favorable resolution of the personal guarantee issue by convincing the lender that it will have to make concessions on this issue in order to win your loan business. This works, particularly in a competitive lending environment, and you should attempt to create that environment. If your business is strong, more than one lender will be interested in your loan business.

A strong earnings history, financial and credit controls, net worth and good management make your business loan more desirable to a lender. If you do not have these credentials try:

1. Asking the lender what it will take to eliminate the personal guarantee.
2. Offering a personal guarantee, but limiting your liability, for example, to 10 percent of the loan principal or a fixed dollar amount.
3. If the business has multiple owners, allocating the guarantee liability on a pro rata basis so each owner is individually liable only for a pro rata share of the personal guarantee; or
4. Offering a guarantee of certain issues. You can address the lender's concerns over accountability for adequate accounts receivable, inventory levels and equipment maintenance without providing your unlimited personal financial guarantee of payment or value.
5. Seeking out another lender.
6. Replacing some or all of the debt with equity by taking in a venture capitalist or other partner.

Remember, when pursuing loans for your privately held business, there is or can be a competitive market for your loan business. You can negotiate the interest rate and other economic terms of the loan. When negotiating with your lender, establish at the outset that the personal guarantee will be a pivotal issue. You may have to make concessions on other loan issues to avoid or reduce your guarantee, but these concessions may be worthwhile in order to protect your family's security and your personal assets. Before negotiating loan terms or signing loan documents, seek the advice of an experienced attorney. The lender's form documents and "boilerplate" language are written to protect the lender and are not designed to favor the borrower.

■ Negotiating the Loan Agreement

All of the negotiation points I've just discussed are ways to chip away at the personal loan guarantee, but the principles of give and take should also be applied when you negotiate the loan itself. Remember, bankers negotiate with entrepreneurs three times a day, but entrepreneurs negotiate with bankers once every few years.

Bankers often work troublesome provisions into a loan agreement. Perhaps you'll think them too strict or unfair, but instead of complaining to your banker, start chipping away at them. There is no such thing as a boilerplate; every item in a loan agreement is negotiable, depending on your situation.

The following is a list of some troublesome loan provisions.

- Five days to advise you of infraction.
- One week to cure a default.
- Bank mistakes against you to which you fail to call attention within 30 days are forfeited.
- Bank mistakes in your favor that you don't catch can be corrected by the bank at any time (no time limit).

Negotiate Around Inequitable Provisions

If the bank wants a notice period of five days to advise you of an infraction of the loan contract, ask your banker for ten business days. Or, if your loan agreement offers you a grace period of one week to cure a default, ask to substitute fifteen business days to assure that you'll have enough time after written notice of the default is received.

Also watch for a list of petty technical violations that would put the loan into default. Your loan agreement may prevent you from leasing "capital equipment." Does that include an office copier? Technically, it does, and if your loan officer comes under pressure to trim his loan portfolio, he could use this technicality against you. Loan officers are often beset by bank regulators, and the letter and the spirit of the law can be quite opposite. Make sure the word *material* is used to modify a declaration of default.

Watch for inequitable provisions in the loan agreement and don't hesitate to challenge your banker on them. You may find that bank mistakes against you to which you fail to call attention within 30 days are forfeited while bank mistakes in your favor that you don't catch can be corrected by the bank at any time. Ask your banker to delete or modify such provisions. You can also negotiate exceptions for restrictions placed by the loan agreement on your working capital. Let's say the agreement requires you to maintain net working capital of $250,000 at all times, but your business experiences a slump in inventory every April. Ask your banker for a 30-day suspension of the provision during that time.

If you practice these examples of how to use the principle of chipping away on your loan agreement, you'll be an expert negotiator by the time you reach the personal loan guarantee!

Seek Legal Advice on Financial Disclosure

One more thing: don't offer to fill out your bank's preprinted personal financial statement. If you do, you are tacitly agreeing to sign the personal loan guarantee. Let your banker raise the subject. When he does, remind him of the value of the assets already included in your business plan. Do not fill in the bank's forms for personal finances. Substitute a signed and notarized form you've prepared ahead of time that gives the same level of information.

Talk to your lawyer before filling out the financial statement. You pay your lawyer high fees: Use him for advice early on because the fees become higher if you get into trouble. Find out from your lawyer how much information you can withhold while staying within the bounds of generally accepted legal procedure. If putting down that expensive second home bothers you, maybe it's time to sell it and put the money into your business. Here is some information your attorney may also find useful.

Banks Must Protect Their Interests, Too

In a reversal of the norm, a federal bankruptcy judge granted unsecured creditors a higher priority in bankruptcy than a bank that lent money for a leveraged buyout.

In the Boston case, Meritor Savings Bank of Philadelphia provided more than $8 million in loans to finance the 1987 leveraged buyout of O'Day Corporation, a Fall River, Massachusetts, manufacturer of fiberglass sailboats. O'Day was a subsidiary of Lear Siegler, Inc. Less than two years later, the unsecured creditors forced the company into involuntary bankruptcy.

After a week-long bench trial, U.S. bankruptcy judge James N. Gabriel of Boston ruled that the bank loans constituted a fraudulent conveyance because

Meritor had reason to know that the transaction would leave the company insolvent.

In the ruling, Judge Gabriel found that O'Day was left with only $1,300 in cash after paying all of the costs associated with the buyout. He said Meritor knew that the financial projections for O'Day's performance after the buyout were inaccurate and that the transaction would fail.

While ruling that the bank didn't intend to defraud the creditors, Judge Gabriel nonetheless wrote that the bank "set out on a course to improve its own position to the serious detriment of the unsecured creditors" after the company ran into financial difficulties. He did allow the bank to retain its security interest in real estate to pay down $1,380,000 that was lent to O'Day after the buyout. Meritor's appeal is pending.

Mancuso's 15 Ways To Improve Your Banking Ability

Today, the equity markets have become tighter and the debt markets looser. There is less venture capital available since the market crash, and the banks have more money to lend. Hence, it's not surprising to find entrepreneurs now seeking to raise capital from their friendly banker. Here are a few techniques and tips for being more successful in locating a good bank and a great banker.

1. Never pick a bank, always pick a banker. The individual you work with is usually more important than the institution you choose.

2. The best way to find a good banker is to ask for a referral from a successful entrepreneur. The nicest thing a customer can do for a banker is to offer a good referral.

3. Don't use your corporate lawyer to negotiate a loan. Find a lawyer who represents a competing bank and retain that law firm for your negotiations. Obviously, they'll be familiar with the issues, and your negotiating power will increase perceivably when you use a competitor's legal counsel. However, do all the negotiating yourself.

4. Try not to fill in the bank's forms for personal finances. Rather, substitute a signed and notarized form that you prepared ahead of time, which gives the same level of information. Do not inflate personal financial statements, as false statements can come back to haunt you.

5. In addition to knowing your loan officer and his background, become familiar with the bank. Know what's hot and what's not. Real estate? The middle market? What is the bank seeking to specialize in? From annual reports or quarterly statements, you can usually find out where the prob-

lem loans are. Most likely the bank will be timid about lending in that area for a few years. This can be vital information.

6. From the bank's financial information, determine its loan-to-deposit ratio, a key indicator of its lending aggressiveness. If it's climbing, the bank is lending, and if it's shrinking, the bank isn't lending. The ratio usually runs about 60 to 70 percent. (At urban banks, the ratio may be higher.)

7. Banks typically claim that for every one dollar they have in assets, they like to lend out 60 cents and keep 20 cents in cash and 20 cents in secondary reserves, which can be made liquid in one or two days. How does your bank check out on these ratios?

8. A banking rating service can supply you with a report on any bank, analyzing its strength. It can give you details not commonly accessible, because its information comes from regulatory agencies that monitor banks. For instance, it can tell you the level of Third World debt or insider loans. (See Appendix for listings.)

9. The Harvard Business School has an excellent case analysis of the New Venture Group at the Bank of Boston. Contact: Publishing Division, Harvard Business School, Soldier's Field, Boston, MA 02163. Ask for case #9-286-070, by W.A. Sahlman. The cost is ($10).

10. A good bet might be an SBA-guaranteed loan—as much as $750,000 for a term of seven years. Call the SBA field office nearest you or call the SBA Answer Desk at 800/827-5722.

11. Banks are receptive small business owners who are knowledgeable and well prepared. Submitting a written business plan with your loan request makes you an above-average candidate.

12. Your accountant is the crucial link to your banker. If your banker and your accountant don't like or trust each other, your chances of getting a loan are slim.

13. Not everyone has to personally guarantee corporate bank debt, but banks will tell you that everyone does. Your task is to find small business owners who borrow without personal guarantees, and then determine what they have that you don't.

14. The only time to raise capital is when you don't need it. Bankers prefer to lend money to customers who have borrowed before and have paid back at least one loan on time. This encourages entrepreneurs to have accounts at multiple banks and multiple banking relationships.

15. Try foreign-owned banks to secure debt. In 1990, they expanded their commercial and industrial loans by 18 percent. And foreign doesn't mean

10,000 miles away. The Canadian Imperial Bank of Commerce expanded its loan volume by one-third in 1990. Japanese banks are better capitalized than American banks and will continue to prosper as the regulations on bank capital tighten. The cheaper dollar, down 15 percent against most major currencies since the summer of 1990, helps stretch bank capital allocation in foreign currencies.

■ The Crazy Things Entrepreneurs Do

Lenders have no idea how personal loan guarantees can pressure an entrepreneur into doing crazy things, most of which are not good for the company or the bank. A California entrepreneur had a $1.3 million personal loan guarantee on his business loan and he had about $1.5 million of personal assets. When the business began failing, the bank pressured him about the house and more collateral. He began discussions with his lawyer.

According to the entrepreneur, the lawyer strongly recommended that he and his wife "fake" a divorce. Because California is a community property state and because the wife had not guaranteed the bank debt, the lawyer believed he could move assets before any foreclosure.

On that advice, coupled with intense pressure, he and his wife legally divorced and she got most of the assets. He felt he had at least protected his retirement while he continued struggling to save the company. His legal fee for the divorce was $17,000.

The bank rightfully filed a lawsuit for fraudulent conveyance and aggressively sought to set aside the divorce. As the court dates approached the entrepreneur faced the prospect of his parents and children being forced to say in a court of law that he and his wife were divorced.

That could be perjury and he gained a little wisdom and backed down from the lawsuit. This lawsuit cost him $18,000 in legal fees. That's $35,000, so far. So, what we now have is an entrepreneur who loves his wife, from whom he is legally divorced, running a failing business. The story's not over yet, as he is struggling even harder to save the business.

If you go away with just one thought from this chapter, I hope it will be that, just like the rest of us, a banker is a human being and, like any human being, responds to warmth and friendly interest. Do your research and have all the facts and figures you need, but don't forget to treat your banker as you would any friend from whom you want a favor. Be her best customer, and you'll get off those personal loan guarantees. *And remember, the best way to get off a personal loan guarantee is not to sign the damn thing in the first place!*

■ ■

8

How To Negotiate

I put a chapter in this book on the subject of negotiating to make your job a little easier. Throughout the process of starting or acquiring a business of your own, you will undoubtedly ratchet upward in your negotiating abilities. It will be one of the major changes between a corporate and entrepreneurial existence.

When dealing in the world of entrepreneurs and CEOs, you will be working with mirages, miracles and magic. What seems to be true will be false and vice versa. I've excerpted some of my previous book, *Winning with the Power of Persuasion* (Dearborn, 1993) here because I believe it can act as a grease to make the transition less painful.

■ Linking Old Truths to Create Leverage

Most good, practical ideas, especially in negotiations, were thought up a long time ago by the Greeks and Romans. Very few new ideas are really new. Maybe we can count Einstein's theory of the relationship between mass and energy as one, but can you tell me another? Really, what today's great thinkers do is link old truths in new ways. Most new ideas are a repackaging of various portions of old ideas, taking a bit from each to form a totally new concept.

I recently had an impacted wisdom tooth removed. Afterwards, the oral surgeon told me to put medicine in the empty socket every other day. I asked if it was a new genetically engineered high-tech drug to stop the pain. He smiled and said it was good old-fashioned clove, which has been the solution to this problem for several thousand years. So far, he said, nobody has found anything better than this herb to heal an open wound in the mouth.

Few concepts in this book are new, but when they are packaged this way they become new. In fact, many of these ideas may be so old that rereading them here may be nothing more than remembering what you have forgotten. But that makes them new, too. This should not lessen their impact, but rather strengthen it. When we forget something and then recall it after a long absence, it creates a bond that is stronger than when you first accepted it as truth. It's like renewing an acquaintance with an old friend. It happens faster, and when it's done repeatedly its intertwining linkages make it a stronger bond.

So don't accept anything here as new, but as tried and true. The fundamental truths stand the test of time.

The Art of War*

The best book of strategy was compiled over 2,000 years ago by a mysterious Chinese warrior philosopher, Sun Tzu. It's called the *Art of War,* but it has been eagerly adopted by modern military people. In fact, General (Stormin') Norman Schwartzkopf, who led the forces against Iraq, was a long-time fan of Sun Tzu's philosophies.

Some see in the successes of postwar Japan an illustration of Sun Tzu's dictum of the classic "to win without fighting is best." The concepts in this classic get better over time.

Many corporate executives think of settling a dispute as something akin to verbal boxing. You pound through your arguments until you get what you want. Much more elegant and effective models are the Oriental martial arts, like aikido and t'ai chi. There, the goal is not to overcome force, but to redirect it—not to meet force with force, but to align yourself with the force directed at you and guide it in a new direction.

The best soldier does not attack. The superior fighter succeeds without violence. The greatest conqueror wins without a struggle. The most successful

---

*Michael Crichton dedicated his best-selling book *Rising Sun* to the Japanese motto "Business is war." Throughout the book, he claims that subterfuge is the normal way of doing business Japanese-style.

manager leads without dictating. This is called intelligent nonaggressiveness. This is called mastery of men.—Lao-Tsu, *Tao the King*

Here is a sample of a few of the philosophies expressed by Sun Tzu. You'll find these helpful as you prepare for a new career in your own business.

- "All warfare is based on deception."
- "Offer the enemy a bait to lure him; feign disorder and strike him."
- "In war, numbers alone confer no advantage. Do not advance relying on sheer military power."
- "The enemy must not know where I intend to give battle. For if he does not know where I intend to give battle, he must prepare in a great many places. And when he prepares in a great many places, those I have to fight in any one place will be few."
- "For to win 100 victories in 100 battles is not the acme of skill. To subdue the enemy without fighting is the acme of skill."
- "Thus, what is of supreme importance in war is to attack the enemy's strategy."

Now do you see why I like to say most of the really good concepts were thought up years and years ago?

Attila the Hun

Attila, king of the Huns, was born in a chariot somewhere in the valley of the Danube River around the year 395 A.D. He was the son of King Mundzuk and could trace his ancestry for some 32 generations. When he became king, he controlled an army of 700,000 warriors, mostly barbarians. He shaped an aimless hoard of mercenary tribal nomads into the undisputed rulers of the ancient world.

Attila's legacy is not as well known to the Western world as Alexander the Great or Caesar or, for that matter, Ivan the Terrible. But his legacy was that of a mighty king whose goodness and wisdom had no equal. His story is told in detail in a little book by Wess Roberts, *The Leadership Secrets of Attila the Hun* (Warner, 1985).

America's most outspoken and visible entrepreneur, H. Ross Perot, of EDS fame, is recognized as the high priest of entrepreneurs. Attila "the Hun" Ross, is the Texan (yes, another of them) who was so outspoken about how to run the country and who gave his boss, Roger Smith, fits after he sold EDS for billions to General Motors. Perot once infuriated Smith by trying to give out 500 copies of leadership secrets at a dinner attended by the managers of GM's new Saturn division. Maybe you should emulate both Ross and Attila.

Machiavelli

Another ancient masterpiece still popular today has guided heads of countries. Over 400 years ago, a Florentine statesman named Machiavelli wrote a book called *The Prince,* in which he set down the rules of politics. Machiavelli's work (which sprang up at a time when democracy was not in vogue) is often viewed as a blueprint for dictators. But *The Prince* is much more than that. And the modern-day persuader can find plenty that applies to managing a business in Machiavelli's insights.

A Machiavelli Sampler:

- "The first impression that one gets of a ruler and of his brains is from seeing the men he has about him."
- "A prince need trouble little about conspiracies when the people are well disposed, but when they are hostile and hold him in hatred, then he must fear everything and everybody."
- "A prince must show himself a lover of merit, give preferment to the able and honor those who excel in every art."
- "A man who wishes to make a profession of goodness in everything must necessarily come to grief among so many who are not good."
- "Therefore, it is necessary to learn how not to be good, and to use this knowledge and not use it, according to the necessity of the case."
- "There is no other way of guarding one's self against flattery than by letting men understand they will not offend you by speaking the truth."

Archimedes

Archimedes was an ancient philosopher who discovered the fundamental law of leverage. You might say his work spawned the leveraged buyout craze, which led to the junk bond market, which contributed to the $500 billion savings and loan bailout. Bank debt, Drexel Burnham and Michael Milken are just icons following a basic law that was developed centuries ago.

Archimedes once said: "If you give me a lever long enough and allow me to stand on the other side of the moon, I could use the lever to move the earth." He was technically right. If you have enough leverage, you can do anything, even move the earth.

Basically, you have two ways to increase your leverage: either lengthen your lever, or move your fulcrum closer to the object you want to move.

Old Is Better Than New

The brain naturally rejects anything new. It's an immune system response to an outside invader. All the brain cells come together to keep out change or novel ideas. Remember, the Catholic Church excommunicated Galileo because he said the earth traveled around the sun.

But when persuasion is said to be nothing more than the three old truths of negotiating, selling and motivating mixed together in a new way, it's like an old lost friend, and it's greeted with warmth and acceptance.

■ Fundamental Negotiating Concepts

Roger Dawson sells both a live seminar ($495) and a set of six audio cassettes ($39.95) called the Secrets of Power Negotiating. He also throws in 24 Power Negotiating Ploys on flash cards. His tapes are offered by the best source of audio cassettes I have found—Nightingale Conant (7300 N. Lehigh Ave., Chicago, IL 60648, 708/647-0300).

Dawson promises you will learn to:

- Get your kids to go to bed without a hassle.
- Get a hotel room after 6:00 p.m. when the sign says "No Vacancy."
- Get the price of a "loaded" car down to 20 percent above dealer cost—with the extras thrown in for free.

Herb Cohen—Master Negotiator

Another ancient principle of negotiation has been popularized by Herb Cohen of the Power Negotiation Institute in Skokie, Illinois. Herb is a stand-up comedian á la Henny Youngman, who delivers very practical, straightforward negotiating advice that's built around the laws of human behavior. He has appeared on TV quite often (Larry King) and is the author of the best-selling book, *You Can Negotiate Anything*. His advice is "to care, but not that much."

What Cohen means is that when you become obsessed with a negotiation, there is less chance to arrive at a reasonable solution because you care so much you can no longer be reasonable. That's why he likes to have third parties handle all negotiations.

In fact, when I arranged for him to speak to the CEO Clubs, never once during the negotiations did Herb enter into the discussion. He had a third party handle all the negotiations. I like people who follow their own advice.

He likes to emphasize this point with a story. He says, "When I'm paid to do a negotiation, I care but not that much because I get paid no matter the outcome. And I am more effective because of it."

I think he's right. Entrepreneurial persuaders are always more effective in highly emotional negotiations by letting others deal directly with the other side. It gives them a leg up because it removes one level of emotion.

How would it be if the president of the United States actually negotiated directly with his Russian counterpart? When these two heads of state meet, they do so not to negotiate, but to ratify what has already been negotiated.

■ Win, Lose or Draw?

Win-Win-Win Negotiations

Another old favorite technique used by entrepreneurial persuaders is to negotiate a win-win settlement. Negotiation is a way of life, and there is no reason a negotiation has to be a win-lose proposition. In fact, it's really better when it is viewed as a win-win-*win* proposition because negotiations that are concluded in this manner stay together. How many times have you seen a win-lose divorce negotiation that eventually comes apart because one side skips town? Who really wins in those cases?

Three levels of wins are necessary for a win-win-*win* negotiation: The universe as a whole has to win (that means everyone on earth), as well as both parties. Here is an example of what I mean.

In the 1970s and 1980s, when the labor unions negotiated with the automotive manufacturers, both sides happily announced a new wage settlement every year without a strike. There were parties and everyone patted the other on the back and celebrated a win-win deal. That was only two wins, however.

Over those happy years, labor wages in the automotive industry climbed steadily. Unfortunately, productivity did not keep pace. While the labor unions and the automotive people were happy, what was really happening was that labor's wages were being passed on to consumers in the form of higher priced cars. The Japanese soon noticed that there was a disparity in the U.S. automotive market and that the prices of American cars were too high. This left a gap they were able to fill with lower-based wages and better manufacturing efficiency. So, what may appear on the outside to have been a win-win negotiation has to become a win-win-*win* negotiation to win in the long term. Persuaders are more effective because they understand this need before the negotiation process begins and they take it into account from the very beginning.

Winning with Concessions

Most folks would agree that Trammel Crow of Dallas is one of the most successful real estate developers. This business requires negotiating skills like few others. It's the showcase of negotiations.

One of Trammel's jewels is worth repeating. After any negotiation, but particularly after a long or bitter one, he waits one day—not two or three, but one. *He then makes one more concession to his opponent.* Obviously, this one wasn't coerced; it was given voluntarily after the agreement was signed. It's a touch of class, but he cautions others not to think about this maneuver or to factor it into the negotiations as it could destroy your ability to conclude a deal.

Win-Lose Negotiations

The choices in a zero sum game are interdependent. What you get is precisely what the other person doesn't get. It's a win-lose proposition, like the classic decision of King Solomon when two women claimed to be the mother of one baby. Solomon's decision to cut the baby in half triggered the love of the real mother, who volunteered to give the baby to the other woman rather than see it killed.

A win-lose negotiation is not the best approach, but it is preferable to a lose-lose negotiation. The division of assets in a divorce or a split-up of a 50–50 company are good examples of situations in which no one wins.

The Texas Draw

Hence, the solution to impossible problems requires innovative and creative approaches. One of the best approaches is called the Texas draw. It's wonderful for zero sum games, and it fits the book's dedication to the spirit of Texas.

Here's how it works: First, one side sets the price; then the other side has the first option to buy at this price for a specified time period. If the buyer accepts the price but fails to exercise the purchase within another specified time period, he or she must forfeit a nonrefundable deposit. How many divorces could be solved if the Texas draw was substituted for lawyers?

One of our lifetime CEO Club members in San Francisco, the late John Regan of insurance fame, had a Texas draw with his parent company. Because two owners of the business had differing views on how to run it, they always had the right to exercise their Texas draw. In Regan's case, it happened once a year during the month of January. It's not perfect, as in Regan's case it eventually resulted in long, expensive litigation, but it's better than the absence of an agreement on how to dissolve.

The Texas draw is similar to the old principle used over the centuries by parents dividing a pie among children. Eventually, the solution gravitates to the choice that allows one child to cut the pie and the other to select the first piece. Again, it is not a perfect solution because children eventually learn that it's better to be the picker than the cutter, but it's better than no agreement.

Ready, set, draw.

■ Negotiating Tips

Choose a Worthy Opponent

I have asked many entrepreneurial negotiators who they would rather negotiate against: an experienced negotiator or an inexperienced negotiator. You might think they would choose inexperienced opponents so they could dazzle them with their footwork, but you'd be wrong. They unanimously prefer to negotiate with experienced negotiators.

Why? Well, first of all, inexperienced negotiators might have to actually make good on all their bluffs. That is dangerous!

Second, isn't the goal of a win-win-*win* settlement more likely if both sides are tuned to the same frequency right from the beginning? Oriental persuaders know this intuitively, but Americans learn it the hard way. The Oriental mind takes longer to negotiate a settlement, whereas the American mind wants to get it done in a ready-fire-aim fashion. The American mind likes to get close and then say, "Let's split the difference." The Japanese like to wait until everyone is fully satisfied. It's quite a difference.

When the rich person meets an experienced person in a negotiation, the experienced person gains a little money and the rich person ends up with a little more experience.

Use Leaders and Trailers

One of the most effective ways to make a statement is to add to it a phrase I call a *leader* or a *trailer.* Take the statement and sandwich it between both a leader and a trailer and you have a persuasive statement that is actually a question. Here are a few of each:

Leaders

"Would it be important to you...?" "Is it feasible to...?"
"Am I safe in assuming...?" "What would be...?"
"If there were a way...?" "Does it make sense to...?"
"Would you have an interest in...?" "What you're really...?"
"Could you suggest...?" "When do you think...?"
"Would you consider...?" "Is a more effective...?"
"Have you ever tried...?" "What would be the best way to...?"

Trailers

"Is that correct?" "Is that important?"
"Am I right?" "Is that accurate?"
"Doesn't it?" "Is that on target?"
"Couldn't it?" "Is that realistic?"
"Shouldn't it?" "Is that pertinent?"
"Wouldn't it?" "Is that relevant?"
"Isn't it?" "Is that clear?"
"Does that make sense?" "Is that what you needed?"
"Fair enough?" "Would that be comfortable?"
"Do you agree?" "Do you understand?"

Negotiate for the Future

Another favorite ploy of an entrepreneurial persuader is to negotiate for something the other party can afford to give up. Never negotiate a nonnegotiable demand. Always negotiate for some small victory before you tackle the tough stuff. That way, you'll at least make a little progress.

When you negotiate, the secret is to make the pie bigger so there can be more opportunities to exchange value. When you view the pie as a fixed size and argue about the percentages being divided among the negotiators, you are already in a trap. A bigger pie gives many more opportunities and the ultimate opportunity to conclude with a win-win-win settlement.

A good technique for making the pie bigger (if you have exhausted all others) is to include the future. All sports teams have made the future a part of their trades and thereby made famous the so-called "player to be named later," which means, "We had a deal and it wasn't quite right so we threw in the adjusting player to be named later." Trading future draft choices is another example of using the future to conclude current negotiations.

For an example a little closer to home, assume that your college alma mater calls and asks you to volunteer to return to the school for a week to head a fundraising campaign for telemarketing to alumni. If they ask you to do it in two or three weeks, you will probably refuse. But if they ask you to do it nine months from now, on a Tuesday, and offer to pay the expenses, they will be more likely to get you. *That shows you are more willing to accept something for the future than you are right now.* That's a very important negotiating principle that all persuaders know intuitively.

A few months ago, I put this principle to work in a negotiation with my landlord. I rent a penthouse for my business in Manhattan. It's in a spectacular setting with panoramic views of the city and a 4,000-square-foot outdoor terrace with trees and a swimming pool. It is the headquarters for my two associations, the Center for Entrepreneurial Management (CEM) and the Chief Executive Officers Club. I like to say I have no desire to leave as I'm on top of the world. Members come from all over the world to party at the penthouse.

However, being on the 17th floor with only one elevator accessible to this penthouse has some disadvantages. There was a major elevator renovation in the building a few months ago. This deprived me of an elevator for more than half a year. It created a serious disruption in service and was a violation of the lease agreement. However, when the new elevator was eventually installed it improved the service to this floor considerably. The landlord and I had a long negotiation over the fact that my service was disrupted during this long period of repair, but we couldn't agree on a reduction in rent. Neither wanted to go to court and leave the settlement in the hands of an unknowing party.

The compromise solution acceptable to both of us was to extend CEM's lease on the space. The logic is beautiful. There was a one-year disruption of service during the ten-year lease. Rather than try to find an economic justification for just how much that is worth, or going to court to fight to see who wins, after some negotiation, CEM and the landlord agreed to extend the lease for another year. That way, CEM had ten good years and one bad year. The period when the elevators were under repair was swapped for a good year in the eleventh year. Winning now was factored against winning later. This is an example of using the future to solve an existing negotiation.

Entrepreneurs know how to expand the pie by making it bigger before it has to be carved up.

■ Mirroring—Believable, Likeable, Trust (BLT)

Isn't it nice when people approach the parent of a new baby and say, "Gee! She looks just like you!" Between you and me, all babies tend to look alike, but don't the parents beam when you see a resemblance!

People like people to look like them, act like them and talk like them. When strangers talk with an accent, we say they talk "funny." The same holds when they look different. We are most comfortable with the familiar, like an old pair of shoes, slippers or an old raincoat. They're like friends.

Funny-looking people come from where you have never been. The funny thing is that you are funny-looking to them, too. The reason we call people we haven't met *strangers* is that they look strange to us.

Mirroring—I Like You

One of the most effective techniques of a persuader is mirroring. What it says, in essence, is that when someone behaves like you, you like them better. When you like them, you are more prone to follow them or to do things they like to do. They become a pied piper to you. It's an old truth.

The great hypnotherapist, Dr. Milton Erickson, learned to mirror the breathing patterns, posture, tonality and gestures of other people. And by doing that, he achieved a binding rapport in a matter of minutes. People who did not know him suddenly trusted him without question.

When you watch an entrepreneur persuading another person, observe how often he mirrors the other person in a natural way. When the entrepreneur removes his glasses, the other person removes or touches his glasses. When the other person scratches, the entrepreneur scratches. Mirroring is a natural act of an entrepreneurial persuader.

So how do you mirror another person? What kinds of physical traits can you mirror? Start with the voice. Mirror the person's tonality, phrasing, pitch, pace, pauses and volume. Mirror favorite words or phrases. How about posture and breathing patterns, eye contact, body language, facial expressions, hand gestures or other distinctive movements? Any aspect of physiology, from the way a person plants his feet to the way he tilts his head, is something you can mirror.

People feel as though they've found their soulmate—someone who totally understands, who can read their deepest thoughts, who is just like them. But you don't have to mirror everything about a person to create rapport. If you just start with the tone of voice or a facial expression, you can learn to build incredible rapport with anyone.

Let me give you an example. Have you ever been sitting in a restaurant alone with a newspaper when you noticed someone else sitting in another booth reading the same newspaper? As dinner progresses, it seems that this person is turning the pages at about the same frequency as you; in fact, he is reading the same articles. You are speaking to the waitress at about the same frequency, and, lo and behold, when you get up to go to the bathroom, he follows.

Did it ever happen that this person eventually approaches you and says, "You know, you look familiar. Do we know each other?" What's been happening is that you have been mirroring each other. When you mirror someone, you become familiar, and when you become familiar to that person, you become liked because we like people and things with which we are familiar. Simple, isn't it? In fact, mirroring is a very effective technique for meeting someone you want to meet. If you behave the way the other person does, it increases the likelihood that you will cross paths.

■ Nonverbal Communication

Ninety-three percent of all communication is nonverbal. Yet, ninety-three percent of most preparation is spent on the verbal portion of communication. When you want something to happen, your whole being has to want it. The words you say are never as important as the way you say them. Just remember, you can say "*I* love you,", "I *love* you", or "I love *you*."

Studying nonverbal communications and being sensitive to signals radiating form the other communicator is one of the key skills of an effective persuader. An excellent book on the subject is *Metatalk: How to Uncover the Hidden Meaning in What People Say* by Gerard Nierenberg (Negotiation Institute, 341 Madison Ave., New York, NY 10017, 212/986-5555). It's a little handbook with visual detail and pictures for various methods of nonverbal communication. He doesn't discuss gestures, but clusters of gestures. For example, when your arms are folded and legs crossed, it usually means that your mind is closed. When your arms and hands are open wide, your heart is open, and your mind is probably open, too.

Too few people recognize how to read nonverbal communication. We concentrate on writing a speech and getting the words right instead of the meaning. It's easier, but not nearly as effective.

■ The Most Powerful Three-Letter Word in This Book Is Ask

If there was a three-letter word that guaranteed:

- the key to winning the law of averages
- magic advice from mentors

- perceived equality from professionals
- increased marketing results
- better marital and family relations
- increased wealth
- positive publicity
- savings on purchases
- the power of a persuader with a purpose

you'd probably want to know this word, wouldn't you? Well, the word is *ask*:

*A*sk and it shall be given.
*S*eek and ye shall find.
*K*nock and the door shall be opened.

The foundation of early thought was the teaching of the ancient Greek philosopher, Socrates. His method of instruction, called the Socratic method, was based solely on the art of asking questions. (Assumptions and analysis were later added to the art of questioning, but many of today's thinkers believe that assumptions make an *ass* out of *u* and *me*, while analysis is all too *anal*.) Today, games like Trivial Pursuit and Jeopardy are based upon the work of Socrates. The art of questioning remains as powerful as it was in ancient civilization.

A child asks sixty questions a day, but the average college graduate asks two questions a day. One of them is, "Where is the bathroom?" Before you dismiss questioning as kid's stuff, consider these words from Albert Einstein:

The important thing is not to stop questioning. Curiosity has its own reason for existing. One cannot help but be in awe when he contemplates the mysteries of eternity of life, of the marvelous structure of reality. It is enough if one tries merely to comprehend a little of this mystery every day. Never lose a holy curiosity.

If You Want To Sell, Ask, Don't Tell

Inc. magazine named Steven Jobs, the founder of Apple Computer and NEXT, entrepreneur of the decade. They also said Mitchell Kapor, founder of Lotus Development Corporation and new president of On Technology, was the best entrepreneur in the software business. My vote for both would go to Bill Gates of the Microsoft Corporation. My reasoning is based upon a statement from Brad Silberberg, Microsoft's vice president in charge of the Windows development program. He said: "Bill Gates has the laserlike ability to home in on the absolute right question to ask. He'll know some intricate lower-level detail about a program and you wonder, 'How does he know that?' Some code or piece of technology Microsoft is not even involved in."

To emphasize the importance of questioning, I recall an incident when I stepped into a men's room off the lobby of the Ritz Carlton Hotel at Laguna Beach. As I was sitting in the stall, I noticed to my chagrin there was no toilet paper. I could see a pair of expensive shoes sitting in the next stall, so I tapped lightly on the partition and asked my neighbor, "Excuse me, do you have any toilet paper in your stall and could you pass it under the partition for me?" The answer came back, "No, I am in the same pickle you are. No toilet paper in here either."

Then I ratcheted the level of concern one notch and asked, "Excuse me, you don't happen to have any old newspapers or legal briefs in that stall with you, do you?" The answer came back, "No, I already told you, I'm in the same predicament you are and I don't know what I'm going to do, either." Obviously, I was still not at the optimum level of questioning. I had wasted two questions and was no better off than when I began.

A minute or two passed and I asked the third and final question in this carefully sequenced "cluster query": "Excuse me, do you have change for a twenty dollar bill?"

Entrepreneurial persuaders accomplish more because they are superstars at asking the right questions at the right times. *This is the key to persuasion and you can never do it often or well enough. You can never be too thin, too rich or ask enough questions. If you don't ask, the answer is no.*

Questioning Techniques

Everyone agrees that the heart of the persuasive process is questioning, but not everybody tells you how to ask better questions.

My vote for the best questioner on television goes to the detective in the rumpled raincoat, Lieutenant Columbo, played by Peter Falk. This supersleuth has been America's favorite detective for the past 20 years, and he always figures out "who done it!"

To see how he does it, write down the questions Columbo asks and number them sequentially. Underline and star the last question he always asks in a sequence. That's the one where he holds one of his arms in the air and says, "Oh, I almost forgot...." This last-minute gesture diminishes the importance of this all-important question. It's always the key question, but he makes it look like an afterthought. When you analyze only Columbo's questions, you'll see question sequences, question clusters and the same questions asked a dozen ways to see if the answers could be different. This is how the little Italian genius finally solves the riddle of "who done it."

■ Ted Levitt—Marketing Guru

In my opinion, the most persuasive management thinker of our time is the colorful Theodore "Ted" Levitt of the Harvard School of Business. He was my marketing guru years ago while I studied at the feet of a master. Looking back over all my education, so much of it was wasteful, but every moment with Ted Levitt was a learning opportunity. That's two years of an MBA plus a bonus year as a research assistant. If you want to read clever thinking and marketing reasoning, read him in the *Harvard Business Review* (he was the editor during the last years of his career) or any of his numerous books. His newest book, *Thinking about Management* (Macmillan, 1991), begins the inside jacket cover with this sentence: "Few things are more important for a manager to do than ask simple questions."

Here are a few examples of good questions for day-to-day situations:

- Meeting a stranger while jogging:
  —How does this track compare to other tracks?
  —How often do you run here?
  —What time did you start?
- Best friend's son's wedding:
  —Do you know the bride or groom?
  —How did you meet?
  —Do you know...?
- Fundraising dinner:
  —What did you do in the campaign?
  —Why are you supporting this cause?
  —Do you know anyone who needs my help?
- CEO Club luncheon:
  —When did you join this group?
  —Do you know many of the members?
  —What other associations do you support?
- At a CEO Club national program:
  —What business are you in?
  —Are you the CEO?
  —Did you start the business?

- Calling on a new prospect in the office:
  —Is that a picture of you?
  —Is this a new office?
  —How's business?
- Visiting a client after the sale:
  —How are things going?
  —Has it lived up to its promise?
  —Do you know anyone else who could use this product?

■ Asking the Right Question Is Only Half the Battle

Asking the right questions in the right sequence is only half the battle. You also have to listen carefully to hear the answer. Failure at either causes failure in communication. Hence, the second most important word in this book and in life is *listen.*

It's not as simple as it sounds, though, because there is a difference between *listening* and *hearing.* For example, my golf pro has told me repeatedly not to look up when I swing. He tells me that at every lesson. I know it cold, and I have no problem with it when I am not at the tee trying to hit the little white object with the big awkward club. But when I swing the club to clobber the ball, I look up a little early. It's not that I don't listen. It's that I don't hear.

Another good example of listening while not hearing occurred during the negotiations that ended the lengthy Vietnam war. Right from the start, you could tell what was going to happen because both sides had completely different attitudes about each other's position. The Americans checked into a posh Paris hotel and set themselves up for a short negotiation. There weren't too many issues as far as they were concerned. The Vietnamese (from a smaller, poorer country), on the other hand, came with only a few people, and the first thing they did was buy a villa just outside of Paris. It comes as no surprise that the two sides couldn't even agree on the shape of the negotiating table. Listening is not hearing.

In negotiations, the real signs of success come not from what is said, but from the way the information is presented: Do the parties speak together? Who speaks first? Do they issue one common statement or two separate ones? These gestures must be heard along with the words.

Entrepreneurial persuaders have better hearing, and in combination with better questioning, they get better results.

■ The Secret To Raising Capital for Entrepreneurial Persuaders

Here's the situation: You've been in a financial negotiation for three months, but the deal just won't close. You've got a terrific business plan—even your venture capitalist admits that—but no matter what you do, you just can't come to terms. So now you're meeting for the umpteenth time, and half of you is thinking, "Maybe I should just get up from the table and leave the room," but the other half is thinking, "I've got three months invested in this deal, they've got the money, they like my plan. I'd be a fool not to stick it out." What do you do? Well, there's a seven-word phrase that will help you close the deal. But before I tell you what it is, I'll show you how and why it works.

The biggest mistake an entrepreneur can make in dealing with a venture capitalist is to lose sight of what every financial source is really after. It may sound like he wants too much equity or too much control, but what it really comes down to is money. His job is to make a profit on his investments. So when the venture capitalist makes what you consider an unreasonable offer ("Just give me my terms and we're ready to go"), you don't have to panic. You don't automatically have to give up control of your business in order to get financed (which is what it may sound like when he says "my terms").

But what do you try next? Do you shop the deal around, hoping to arouse enough interest to play one source off against the other? That might be a good ploy in theory, but in reality shopping a deal around tends to alienate venture capitalists rather than entice them.

Then what's the secret to closing the deal? Is it good old-fashioned persistence? I have always subscribed to the theory that if a batter stands in the batter's box long enough, some dumb pitcher will eventually hit the bat with the ball. But all by itself, persistence won't raise a nickel. It must be combined with persuasion.

Maybe you should try to get the financier to restate everything that attracted him to the deal in the first place. That will bring you back to square one, but it won't get you any closer to closing the deal. That's because as special as you may think your deal, chances are the venture capitalist has seen, and maybe even turned down, similar deals in the past. Getting your business off the ground might be your dream, but the art of raising capital isn't the art of selling dreams. It is the art of reducing risk. Pied pipers know that success in persuasion also requires reducing risk.

The dream sellers will always get into trouble during negotiations because when their backs are up against the wall, they come out and say something like, "You ought to see how beautiful she looks. She's tall and thin and she's got this and that...." But that's not the way raising capital works. In fact, it's just the opposite.

No matter who the investors are, their first concern is getting their initial investment back. So, when a negotiation seems like it's come to an impasse, the seven key words you must say to get the signatures on the agreement are *"You will get your money back first."* That's the magic seven-word phrase.

Here are four examples of why the seven words are magical.

1. Land Sales

About 18 months ago, I bought 100 acres of ocean-front property at Cheboque Point in Yarmouth, Nova Scotia. I paid $100K for this property, but a few months later I needed some cash so I decided to sell off half of it. What do you think the asking price for it was?

If you guessed $100,000, you guessed right. And what this illustrates is perhaps the most important thing to remember about persuading investors: An investor's foremost concern lies in getting his money back. Investors aren't just in the business of making investments. They're also in the business of recouping their investments. It's the way you can tell the good ones from the losers.

2. Gambling

Did you ever watch the gamblers in the casinos in Las Vegas or Atlantic City? Most of them are sensible enough people when they're at home, but put them at a slot machine or a crap table and they go crazy. If you watch long enough, you'll notice that a funny thing begins to happen with some of them. At about two or three o'clock in the morning, they pull all the money out of their pockets and put it down on a table and count it. Then they divide it into two piles and put one of the piles back into their pocket. Then they continue to play with the other pile of money. So what did they put back into their pocket? Cab fare? Money to call home? No. What every smart gambler puts back into his pocket is his initial stake—the money he came with. A fool and his money are soon parted.

3. Venture Capitalist

The best money-raisers in the world are the venture capitalists. Most entrepreneurs have trouble getting someone to cosign a $10,000 note, but a venture capitalist can raise that to the 100th power within an hour.

I speak at a number of conferences where venture capitalists are assembled, and it's always interesting to watch two giants come into the room and meet. And when they do meet, what do you think they say? Does Fred Adler (East Coast) say he made $600 million in the last quarter? Does Arthur Rock (West Coast) say that his average annual rate of return for the past 17 years has been 41.26 percent? No. What they talk about is the success of their *last* fund.

Fred Adler may run four or five different funds of $100 million to $200 million each, but Arthur Rock is only interested in Fred's most current fund. The rest is history. So Fred might say, "I understand you put together $200 million for Fund #6. How long did it take you to get the principal back to your partners in that fund?" and Arthur might answer, "Eleven months." Then Arthur will ask Fred how long it took his last fund to get its principal back to his partners. And so on and so on. *The only thing venture capitalists ever compare is how fast they returned the original investment back to their partners.*

When the gambler puts his original capital back into his pocket, he's doing the same thing as the venture capitalist. He returns the original investment and continues playing on his winnings.

Can you imagine anything more exhilarating than playing with your winnings? It's like funny money. Of course, the venture capitalists are a little more sophisticated. They raise their money in ten-year limited partnerships, but their strategy is the same. They try to rush the original investment back to their partners as soon as possible, and then they play with the winnings for the balance of the ten-year period. The partnership usually has to wait the full ten years to get their winnings, but they get their principal back right away.

4. Initial Public Offering

My last example concerns a young company that goes public at $10 a share. A few months after the initial public offering (IPO) the company runs into some problems, and the stock drops to $5 a share. All of a sudden, the entrepreneur is breaking her back to get the earnings and the stock price back up. After a superhuman effort, the earnings reach, and even begin to exceed, the original projections. But after a slow climb back up, the stock price hits $10 and then just sits there. Why?

Despite the strong performance, the stockholders (investors) remember the initial setback, and when the stock returns to its original price, they begin to bail out. It's what is known as the "jump-off" point. Independent of current performance, the initial investors bail out, and the price gets hung up at its original level. This underscores the same principle I've described in the other three examples: The investor is adamant about recovering the initial investment. In this case, the investor isn't left with any winnings to play with, but at least he's recovered his initial investment and can start over again.

Despite the very different approaches of these four categories of investors— the landowner, the gambler, the venture capitalist and the purchaser of IPO stocks—their thinking is the same: protect the original capital. They all want to make sure the risk on their investment is held to a minimum. They all want to be assured that their original capital will be protected.

Remember, as great as your dream for your company may be, you're on the venture capitalist's turf, so you have to talk his language. So, after you've tried everything you know to close a deal and it still seems to hang up on a few points, try my seven-word phrase: *"You will get your money back first, and then ..."*

■ Negotiating for Control

Persuaders view life as an ongoing series of negotiations, and they must always feel they are in control. In the balance of this chapter, I'm going to show you how to gain control of a negotiation right from the start.

Setting the Opening Conditions

Two of the most successful presenters of negotiation seminars are Chester L. Karrass of California and his son, Gary. They advertise the program extensively, with a headline that says: "In Business You Don't Get What You Deserve, You Get What You Negotiate." One of their central messages, and the subject of Chester's doctoral dissertation, which launched the business, is setting the opening condition. In a simple example of selling a home, Karrass concludes that 90 percent of the sellers do not start with a high enough asking price to allow a successful negotiation that results in the sale of the house. It's a common shortcoming and it's fully understandable.

There is a delicate trade-off of beginning the selling process with too high a price, which could scare off potential buyers, and setting a price that allows room to "give in" to close the sale. According to real estate people, here is how most individuals set the asking price for their home:

- too high   15%
- just right   50%
- too low   35%

The tendency to begin too low outweighs the tendency to set too high by more than two to one. This observation explains why entrepreneurial persuaders succeed where others fail. Entrepreneurial persuaders set the price *too high* about 90 percent of the time. That is dramatically against the flow of the masses. It's not solely because they are optimistic, which they are; it's more an issue of control. They set it too high to stay in control. When you set it too high you *think* you are in control and you act accordingly, but when you set it too low, you *think* you have little control.

The issue of control also comes up in drafting a legal document after a long, drawn-out negotiation. The question is, should you or the other party draw up the agreement? It costs a little more to have your lawyer do it, but it's usually cheaper in the long run. Given a choice, an entrepreneurial persuader will *always* choose to have his or her legal team draw up the papers. Again, it's an issue of control.

This is such a central issue that the legal system tries to even the score by stipulating that, "If a legal issue is vague in the agreement, it will be ruled against the party that drafted it."

When To Mention Price

A related principle of negotiation states that the first party to mention price in negotiation loses. It's the "asking price" question from another angle. It means you should not prematurely announce an asking price because most of the time you will set it too low. It's a good principle, but not infallible.

It works with products advertising as well. Here are two products that offer identical benefits. Which would you rather buy?

- Product 1—$99
- Product 2—$119 to $139, Now $99

Tony Robbins uses this principle in his infomercials. When it comes to selling the books and tapes, the ad usually starts out with the words "Although you'd expect a product like this to cost over $500, we have reduced the price to..." *Persuaders know that value is a perceived concept.*

Ron's Rules for Meetings

The CEO Clubs sponsor a three-day management course that contrasts entrepreneurial and professional management styles. It's conducted in a debate format, and it's a lot of fun. One of the faculty, Ronald Myers, extols the virtues of professional management in the debate. He knows how to gain control in negotiating the terms of his presentation.

Ron prepares the course notebook that contains the notes and copies of overheads used by each speaker. He also drafts the course agenda, and each year he cheats a little to get more time on the podium. Like the entrepreneur who volunteers to draw up the legal papers, Ron knows that by volunteering to draft the agenda he can steal a little control. And, like a true entrepreneurial persuader, Ron sets his asking price too high. He always schedules more than enough time for himself, and it's my job every year to cut back his requests.

Ron understands that entrepreneurs need to be in control in one-on-one or selling situations. The same holds for meetings, so he developed the following groundrules for meetings.

1. *Agree on objectives.* What do we want to have accomplished by the time we walk out of here?

2. *Establish a time frame.* Then let's try to cut it in half. Where meetings are concerned, haste isn't always waste.

3. *Stick to the subject.* Where is this discussion going? What decision are we trying to make?

4. *New input only.* We probably don't need to hear your views several times in order to appreciate their importance.

5. *Bottom line first.* We particularly want your conclusions; we may not need to hear all the reasoning behind them.

6. *One conversation at a time.* We can't afford distractions, and it's unfair to the person whose attention you're borrowing.

7. *No snide remarks.* Someone's feelings could get hurt for no good reason.

8. *Silence is consent.* Speak now, or forever hold your peace.

■ A Final Thought on Control

It's hard, if not impossible, for an entrepreneurial persuader not to be in control. It's the ultimate fear. A symphony conductor has control of over a hundred people simply by the way he moves his hands, but most of us never enjoy that degree of control. To put the issue into perspective, make a list of events you can control and those over which you have no control.

■ No control: death, taxes, weather, traffic...

■ Control: Make your own list.

■ My Favorite Negotiating Lessons

There are several things you should never observe in their formative stages because no matter how good they eventually turn out, the process of making them can be repulsive.

- sausage
- laws
- negotiating lessons
- books

The Big Bluff

This is a true story of the sale of a little company in Sturbridge, Massachusetts, to a big company in Palo Alto, California in 1979.

Coherent Inc, headed by Jim Hobart, chairman, and Hank Gauthier, president, bought a little company called Laser, Inc., headed by Al Battista and Bill Shiner. I had been a founder and a small shareholder and director of Laser, Inc., but I was an adviser, not a player.

One day, the major shareholder, Al Battista, announced he was tired of the problems of being a small company's president and wanted to sell the business. It immediately became my job to sell it. Unfortunately, we had a book value of less than $100,000, and we had not made much money in five years of life. Our sales were under $1 million, but we believed we had good technology and a rosy future.

There was only a handful of potential buyers, and I contacted each of them via a form letter. I think the content has a universal appeal, although it was not entirely true.

We have been approached to sell our business and that's what prompted this letter. While the opportunity presented to us is not perfect, it is acceptable and we are beginning the process to consummate an arrangement.

We are very familiar with (name of company) and your people and your product line. It occurs to us that you and your business would be a better strategic fit for us. However, we do not know if you or your business are possibly interested.

I am handling this situation for the two principals, as I am also a director for the business. Please contact me immediately if you are interested as the process of transferring ownership is already underway.

Please keep this information confidential.

Coherent responded to the letter and arranged for its two principals to visit the company on the evening of an East Coast trip. I picked them up and provided the two-hour ride to and from Boston's Logan Airport to Sturbridge. They spent about six hours in Sturbridge, and during this one and only visit the two persuaders (Hank and Jim) decided to buy the business. Price was not discussed at this meeting. Remember, the first one to mention price loses, so nobody mentioned it. They didn't even drop their guard and ask me in the privacy of the car ride back to the airport.

A few weeks later, Al Battista and I were invited to Palo Alto to negotiate the sale of the business. On the plane, we locked on to a simple strategy we called "the big bluff." Here's how it worked:

- We would say we have an offer now on the table of $1 million.
- We would say we'd rather sell to Coherent because we like the people, the products and the company better. Actually, this was true.
- We would never tell who made the fictitious offer of $1 million.
- We were going to sell the company very soon, possibly in the next month.
- Al and I both had to agree to a deal even though Al had majority control. The other major shareholder, Bill Shiner, did not come to the session because someone had to run the business.

Our justification for not telling all the truth all the time was that we wanted to get the highest price possible for the company. In hindsight, we possibly could have secured the same objectives using different means. But I don't think we would have sold at a cheaper price.

The West Coast meeting began in the Coherent Conference Room and the star of the show was their corporate counsel and a Coherent director, attorney Larry Sonsini. He was a superstar. I had heard of him all the way out on the East coast. Al and I played the role of hillbillies in the presence of such a brilliant luminary. (Actually, we didn't have to act at all.)

Most of the six-hour day was spent with Sonsini at the blackboard doing various financial calculations, showing a fair market value of Laser, Inc. He used book value, market value and liquidation value, and even a generous Sonsini value! No matter how hard he tried, he just couldn't get the value of the business much above $200,000. And this was five times below our asking price of $1 million. After all, Sonsini was working with a balance sheet that had about $100,000 of book value. His numbers were accurate and his approach was fair. He was right and we were wrong.

The day ended, and we had a return flight to catch. We all concluded there would be no deal, as a 500 percent price difference meant we were not even in the same league. We all threw up our hands in frustration as Al and I arranged to leave. As we were boarding the cab, the real decision makers, Hank and Jim, came out to the cab and asked us to stay a little longer. "We'll meet your current offer," they said.

They bought Laser, Inc. for $1 million in 1979, and they overpaid for it significantly. However, one year after the purchase, they both told me it was one of their best long-term investments ever. The company blossomed and Coherent recouped its investment over 1,000 times. In 1992, all the key players were still in place, for Laser, Inc. is now called Coherent General.

The following ten points were mentioned during the negotiations. Each statement is a little negotiating jewel.

1. "Gosh, Mr. Sonsini, that analysis was brilliant, but Mr. Jack Klouts, our neighbor across the street, sold his company for $1 million and it certainly wasn't as good as mine."

2. "I don't know why I want $1 million. I guess there is something magic about big, round numbers."

3. "Is it permissible for Joe and I to be here in the room without a lawyer while you have an attorney present? We don't want to do anything illegal that could overturn the agreement."

4. "I didn't know you were going to bring a bad guy (Sonsini). Our attorney, Dennis O'Connor, is still in Boston. Should we ask him to come out to talk with Mr. Sonsini?"

5. "I don't really know who suggested the $1 million price originally, but that's the offer on the table."

6. "Doesn't it happen that most small companies valued around $1 million actually get sold for $1,000,000? You know, if it's worth $500,000 to $1.5 million, the actual price gravitates towards a million."

7. "I don't really want to negotiate too hard with you now because I'll have to work for you later and I don't want you to think less of me just because of this negotiation. So I'm trying hard to be reasonable."

8. "This is not a lot of money to you, but to us it means life and death."

9. "I'm sorry, but we can't really tell you much about the other offer, just as we can't tell *them* much about you. Do you understand?"

10. "To tell you the truth, we'd really like to sell to you because we like you and your company better. If it was a $10 million sales price, we could afford that luxury. But given the price of only $1 million, we are on the edge of being financially responsible to our families. Once we get rich, we won't have to worry that much about our families."

I share these ten comments because all of them blend logic and emotion. All of them can help you to persuade better, but you must accept the harsh reality that entrepreneurial persuasion incorporates some of the "con." It requires the other party to see things not as they are, but as what you want them to be.

As Karl Vespar, the faculty superstar at the University of Washington in Seattle says, the difference between entrepreneurs and cons is in the degree of long-term value.

The Agent with Limited Authority

One of the most popular negotiating ploys employed by all persuaders is to send an agent with limited authority. Attorney Larry Sonsini was an example of such an agent disguised as a director and adviser to Coherent, which tended to cloud his actual level of authority. You technically can't lose a negotiation when you send an agent with limited authority. After all, limited authority means the agent can't finalize a deal. But that's only in theory.

The best cure for negotiating with such an agent is to ask questions. These questions will help later when the decision makers arrive. Another is to use "the big bluff," as Al and I did in the preceding story.

Attorney Gerard Nierenberg is the founder of the Negotiation Institute in New York City (along with his partner, Richard Zief), and the author of the best negotiating material I have ever read. He traveled with me to all the CEO Club chapters in the late 1980s and offered some classic advice on handling an agent with limited authority. Again, it involves not telling all the truth all the time.

He was going to Los Angeles from New York, but had to stop along the way to give a three-hour seminar in Chicago. He wanted to bring a box of books with him to Los Angeles without the stop in Chicago. When he explained this to the gate agent at the airport, the agent with limited authority said, "Sorry, the baggage must travel with the passenger." Gerry repeated his desire to have the box of books go directly to Los Angeles while he stopped off for a few hours in Chicago, but the agent insisted, "It's against the rules." Dealing with agents with limited authority can be frustrating. They are immune to the music from the pied piper's flute.

Nierenberg handled the agent by using his broad range of baffle. Remembering the most important three-letter word in the world, he approached the agent with a question: "Suppose *you* were going to Los Angeles and had to stop off in Chicago for a few hours, but you wanted your luggage to go directly to Los Angeles—how would you do that?" "Easy," responded the gate agent. "Just come up to me and say, 'I'm going to Los Angeles, and I'm in a hurry. Will you get this luggage to the flight real quick so I don't miss it? I'd sure appreciate it.' Then you can give me your ticket and get a boarding pass after the luggage is gone."

To accomplish more sometimes requires compromise and I'm trying my best to communicate this concept without coming off like a thief. To make it short, simple and memorable, when these persuaders were in grammar school, they almost always had lower scores in conduct than in anything else because they were always pushing the limits of control, even then.

9

All in the Family...
Business

I have included a section on family business in this book because an amazingly high percentage of mid-career executives opt to involve their families in their businesses. It should not be surprising, considering that a person older than 35 is much more likely to have a family than someone just out of school. In fact, if CEM is representative of mid-career executives, about 75 percent of all businesses created by mid-career executives qualify as family businesses. This is a startling percentage, as the number of family businesses in the U.S. population is thought to be below 10 percent. Unfortunately, no reliable hard data exist on this subject and we are forced to make estimates.

Because mid-career executives have acquired both a little money and a little family, they often reason subconsciously that if they add the money to the family, they could operate a little bigger business. It's the old "farmer" mentality of having lots of kids who will provide cheap labor later in life. Plus, there is a certain romance to the old farm system with its stronger family values.

In fact, it's surprising how many mid-career executives do not get into a business, but rather opt to get into a lifestyle. They don't see the business as a vehicle for making money to live a better life, but as an end in itself. They tend to buy country inns in Vermont, ranches out West or sporting centers and health clubs in California. The bad news about almost all of these enviable lifestyle businesses is that they all lose money. They are a luxury for the rich.

■ Famous Family Business Lessons

I'm accepting the reality that a later life entrepreneur will seek to create a family business. That's the given. My goal in this chapter is to share some of my experiences as to the best ways to run such an enterprise. What follows has been excerpted from my book, *How to Run a Family Business* (Simon & Schuster, 1991), coauthored with Nat Shulman of Best Chevrolet in Boston.

As I was writing my family business book, the entrepreneurial heroes of the '80s, Donald and Ivana Trump, were carrying on in their ongoing soap opera—which ran in the *New York Post* for months—"Trump: The Divorce." Just as I began this chapter of this book the entrepreneurial couple of the '90s, Woody Allen and Mia Farrow, started their comedy.

How all this hoopla will affect the children of these marriages nobody knows, but I believe the principles I advocate in this book would help them as surely as they can help your family (which at times may not seem any more sane than the Trumps). The lessons of the Henry Ford or Seward Johnson stories apply to the Trumps, too. And, in turn, to your little candy store!

The creation of an empire requires motivation and commitment bordering on obsession. The folks who create wealth are not always nice people. It's hard to like Donald Trump, perhaps even for his kids. The same goes for Steven Jobs, who married in his thirties, or for cable king Ted Turner, who had several marriages before he found Jane Fonda. Still, almost everyone admires what these people have accomplished, and the same goes for a monstrous father like Henry Ford.

Strong Followed by Weak Followed by Strong

Strong fathers seem to have sons at one or the other end of the spectrum from weak to strong, but never in the middle. Trump, Fred Smith of Federal Express and Howard Hughes were all the offspring of very strong fathers. The legendary insurance great, W. Clement Stone, on the other hand, outlived both his children, neither of whom could follow in his footsteps, and J. Paul Getty's oldest son, once the world's wealthiest man, scorned all business pursuits for a quiet career as an artist.

For the story of Henry Ford's domination of his son, see the section on the Fords in this chapter. H.L. Hunt's children by his first marriage squandered a fortune worth billions of dollars. His children by his second and third marriages did much better with the family fortune and business, bringing to mind a comment I once heard Herb Cohen of the Power Negotiation Institute of Chicago make: "Kids are like pancakes—it's best to throw out the first batch."

Entrepreneurial families tend to follow a pattern of strong, weak, strong, weak, strong, weak through the generations. This pattern holds true for the Johnson family. I suspect we'll begin to see the same pattern with entrepreneurial mothers and daughters. It will be fascinating to see what happens to Donald Trump's children after two generations of strong fathers.

The histories of some of the most famous family businesses in the world are more instructive as examples of how not to have a successful family business. The family businesses I discuss in this chapter share one common problem: success of the business at the expense of the family. And, in the Bingham case, for example, the family disintegration during the buildup of the business becomes the eventual downfall of the business. A family business cannot be deemed truly successful unless both the goals of the business and goals of the family—which are often diametrically opposed—are met.

I have encapsulated some famous stories from the annals of family business history. By examining these real stories, with human blemishes, you can perhaps learn how to avoid the problems they illustrate. All are true stories, as in family business the truth is always wilder than fiction.

- Stew Leonard
- The Corleones
- The Guccis
- The Binghams
- Johnson v. Johnson
- The Fords

■ Stew Leonard's World's Largest Dairy Store

Stew Leonard was a second-generation milkman with a home delivery route until 1968, when Connecticut state highway construction forced him to relocate his dairy plant. With the help of a loan from the Small Business Administration, he built a unique store around a glass-enclosed dairy plant in Norwalk, Connecticut. Twenty-six additions to the original building later, the 106,000-square-foot complex sprawls on eight and a half acres.

Current sales are approaching $100 million at the location in Norwalk alone. An additional store has been opened in Danbury under the direction of son Tom, and other locations are in process. Stew Leonard's was featured in Tom Peters' best-seller *A Passion for Excellence* as one of the best-run companies in America. The store has a country fair atmosphere, with employees dressed as farm animals strolling the aisles to amuse customers, prompting the

New York Times, New York magazine and *Fortune* to refer to Stew Leonard's as a "Disneyland Dairy Store." There are also cows that moo when a child presses a button, two eight-foot dogs who play the banjo and serenade shoppers with country tunes and a farmer who sings and talks to passing children.

The company is a partnership between Leonard and his wife, Marianne. His two sons, Stew, Jr. and Tom, daughters Beth and Jill, two of Leonard's sisters, two brothers-in-law and various other relatives are also part of the team. The Leonards are so convinced of the value of families working together that 55 percent of the 600 people working at the store have at least one relative who also works there.

Stew Leonard, Sr. passed the ball to the next generation several years ago. Stew, Jr. is president of the company, son Tom is in charge of the Danbury store (150 employees), daughter Jill is manager of personnel, and daughter Beth manages the store bakery (aptly called Bethy's Bakery). According to the Food Marketing Institute, this bakery annually sells more than 20 times as much as any other in-store bakery in America.

Stew Leonard, Jr. recounts the following story about his father's near obsession with family in business:

> One time we were all sitting around the dinner table and my father took out four sticks bound together. He set them on the table and asked, 'Who can break these?' Beth and Jill started first and Tommy and I said, 'Ah, that'll be no sweat.' We tried to do it, but we couldn't break the bound sticks, so we handed them back to our father. He then undid the binding holding the sticks together and handed each of us a single stick, saying 'Now try it.' Each one of them snapped easily, but together, they couldn't be broken!

Stew Leonard, Sr., says, "When there are children in the business, there is tremendous loyalty, trust, dependability and feeling of ownership. The disadvantage is that it is very hard to wear two hats as a boss and as a parent."

A manifestation of the "two hats syndrome" happened several years ago with Leonard's younger son, Tom. Tom, then a recent college graduate, wanted time off to drive to Fort Lauderdale for a concert. The boss (Hat 1, Dad) said no, but Tom went anyway. On his arrival home, the boss (Hat 2, Employer) told his employee he was fired. Dad then asked his son how he could help him find a job.

Leonard, Sr., whose father died at age 57, shares:

> When you're young and you're taking over the family business, not a day goes by that you don't wish you could talk to your dad and ask him to explain something.

Don't live your life as though you have 2,000 years before you. That's been our philosophy in our business. My son was made president of Stew Leonard's three years ago. I was only 55 years old. The business was growing and it needed me, but I think that's one of the real challenges for the founder—to hand the baton over to others. There's a little ego involved. You have to adjust to it, you have to see them make mistakes and just bite your bottom lip. But most of all, you need to be a coach and a back patter.

Business can be fun! This is the mainstay of our business from the customer through the team member, to the family member. What we're trying to do is make an experience, especially with our own children here, that success in our line is becoming yourself at your very best. It's got nothing to do with money. It's how you are going to develop. And I always say that if one of our children wanted to become a rock star, Marianne and I would have gladly bought the guitar.

The following conversation with the Leonards throws some light on how the family deals with issues of responsibility, performance and succession.

Q. How do the Leonards resolve family issues and problems?

A. Stew, Sr. We try to departmentalize our business. Beth runs Bethy's Bakery, and she is the undisputed boss. That's her domain, and the other kids have nothing to say about the way she runs it. The same is true for Jill, who runs personnel and human services, and for Tom in the Danbury store. We don't stick our noses in their departments. We let them run their areas, and we judge them by their results. And we're not day-to-day people; we're bottom-line, results-oriented people. And the bottom line does not necessarily mean profit—it means results. Our philosophy has always been, let's build something great and the profits will take care of themselves. We're not profit oriented, and we're not financially oriented. We realize that both are important; however, we happen to be more customer-oriented.

A. Stew, Jr. One thing we try to do is ask how serious the problem is. If it's something we can work out together, we usually try to do that one on one over lunch or dinner. If that doesn't work, sometimes we'll get all the kids together and try to hash it out. And if that doesn't work, we bring in a gavel with Dad and Mom sitting in. Professor John Ward, our consultant, has suggested that we develop a board of directors to help resolve business and family decisions.

Q. How do you assess each family member's performance—their contribution to the numbers?

A. Stew, Sr. It's not a competitive thing to see how well Beth does compared to Danbury or whatnot. We don't compete among ourselves that way. There's no competition among the four children. We're in it together; it's a team effort, and the results are the whole company.

Q.   How do you extend the idea of family and opportunity to nonfamily members in the organization?

A. Stew, Jr. That really gets to the question of evaluating performances. As far as the family goes, we really are performance oriented. Our philosophy is that if you can't measure it, you can't manage it. And we really try to measure a lot of stuff: The cleanliness of our building is measured. Employee attitudes are measured. The performance of groups of people within each of our departments is measured. When you come into the store, it's like the family doesn't really exist anymore. It's a performance thing. The boss of our store is the customer, and that's something everybody is working at. We go to great lengths with our managers and people at the store to make sure that what gets rewarded is performance. We have people who started with us in high school and are making $50,000 to $60,000 after being here about ten years. Other people who have done a great job are up around $100,000. We reward everybody real well because we believe in paying for performance.

A. Stew, Sr. The point is, what gets rewarded gets repeated. We are literally a big happy family, with 55 percent of our staff having a family member working there. So we have to have pretty definite rules about how that's run. One of the things we try is to keep them out of each other's hair. That is, the family member isn't working directly with his or her husband or wife. But we find it a great advantage in one respect, because the business is carried home afterward. The other thing we find is, if the mother recommends her daughter to become a cashier, the daughter not only has me for a boss, she also has her mother.

A. Tom. Opportunity is even greater at Stew Leonard's because there are family members spread throughout the organization. People who are doing a great job are recognized much faster than if there was just one person who was responsible for all the promotions.

Q. How do you handle the succession process from the father to the next generation?

A. Stew, Jr. My father really has tried to relinquish a lot of day-to-day control. He's more of a teacher. I know the hardest part about succession, personally, is that it's one thing to give me the title of president, but nothing changes the day after. You have to earn respect from people, and that sometimes takes years. My father has had some very loyal, great people who built the business up with him. You can't have a junior walking in and expect those people to suddenly take orders from him. Once they gain respect for you, then the succession process is a little bit easier.

A. Stew, Sr. We're great believers in Dale Carnegie. We've sent more than 1,000 people, including all of our family, through Dale Carnegie several times because I think it's an ongoing learning process to be diplomatic about the succession problem—and it is a problem. We have an older relative, Marianne's brother, who has been with me since I started the business. He's a vice president, and he's not going to be president. I remember the day I told him that I decided to make Stew, Jr., the president. He didn't like to hear that, but he has adjusted to it. He doesn't have a choice in that. This isn't a town meeting, it's a family business, and somebody has to run it. And you don't help the thing by delaying it. There's a time when a father has to say, "OK, you're going to run the business." If you can make a smooth transition and let the son earn his stripes, it might even be a better company with him. That's what you're after.

Professor John Ward is director of the family business program at Loyola University in Chicago and one of the foremost family business consultants in the world. He has consulted with the Leonard family for several years and offers these observations on their success:

- Stew Leonard, Sr. has tremendous appreciation for the contributions of his wife. Marianne accepted primary responsibility for rearing the children well and gave her husband a positive, supportive environment.

- Stew, Sr. is not money-driven. Instead, he is driven by personal philosophies and by the challenges of management.

- Stew, Sr. made a commitment to succession planning and attended to it at a very young age. Stew, Jr., is already president of a $100 million business at the age of 32. The future disposition of the company stock has been determined: It will be split equally among the offspring. Stew, Sr. realizes that while the communication and implementation of succession are not flawless, these flaws are best overcome with extra time and parental attention while the parents are still the active family leaders and while the children's career paths and self-concepts are not totally rigid.

- While Stew, Jr. enjoys the title and privilege of president, his brother, brother-in-law and sisters, all of whom work in the business, understand and empathize with the serious responsibility he holds. They don't see it as merely a matter of privilege and perks.

- Stew, Sr. has developed many new passions and activities and feels that they are actually competing with his time at the store. This makes letting go much easier.

- This is a family and a business whose values are extremely important. They are reinforced daily. Many of the same values drive both the business and family life. Most importantly, the values among the four siblings are very homogeneous. In short, the family and business value systems are powerful, congruent, homogeneous and substantially overlapping.

In summary, the Leonard family is an enchanting, exciting clan all working together in the family business. Perhaps their greatest strength is the tremendous thirst they have to learn as individuals and as a family. They read family business literature aggressively. They attend family business conferences and seminars. They are willing to hire family business experts.

The Leonards are my only success story in this chapter, and it's one of the best successes in the world. But I'd be remiss if I failed to also mention a dark cloud on the horizon. The *Hartford Courant* newspaper reported that Stew Leonard, Sr. and several others were indicted for sales tax fraud. At the time of this writing, the issue is unresolved.*

■ Family Business Goes to the Movies: The Godfather

As you are considering a business opportunity that will include your family, let's look at the benchmark family business, the Corleones. By highlighting a few scenes from this romantic version of the life story of one of New York's five crime families, I will uncover the generally accepted folklore about what really goes on in a family business. After all, movies and plays must reflect some degree of truth if they hope to receive wide acceptance.

The dramatic transition of power between the father, Vito Corleone (Marlon Brando), and his son Michael (Al Pacino), who becomes the new godfather, captures some key principles of family business:

---

* As this book was being printed, Stew Leonard, Sr., admitted to stealing $17 million over ten years and agreed to pay a $15 million fine. The September 1993 issue of my newsletter tells the details of this tragedy. He is expected to be sentenced in October 1993 to five years in prison.

1. *The offspring least likely to be a successor usually ends up running the business. Therefore, you can never overtrain even the least likely.* In *The Godfather*, it was always assumed that the oldest son, Sonny Corleone (played by James Caan), would eventually control the business. As the oldest, he was groomed for this control, he was expected to accept it, and he acted as if it were his birthright. The daughter, the middle child among three sons, was never expected to assume a key position in the business. The third son, Freddie, was incompetent and was never considered for the stewardship of the family business. The youngest son, Michael, was as talented as Freddie was untalented. He was judged least likely to enter the family business, so he was excluded from the inner secrets of the business. He was raised to be something special. He went to college and even became a war hero, demonstrating early success outside of the family business.

   The family business situation shifts suddenly when the competition—a rival mob—tries to kill Don Corleone. Michael has to become involved because the attack was not only on the business, but on his father. We see immediately that family and business cannot be separated. In the ensuing strife, Sonny, the heir-apparent, is murdered. The business has to be kept in the family, so Michael inherits control.

   This is a classic case. It often happens that the least likely offspring eventually assumes the stewardship of a family business, so you can never overtrain the least likely. Otherwise, this successor will have to assume an immense burden and intense risk without training.

2. *To make the family business prosper, the successor may have to get rid of the in-laws.* Blood is thicker than water, and these days blood is certainly thicker than marriage. It is difficult to be an in-law in a family-controlled business because one's tenure is often contingent upon the success of the marriage.

   In *The Godfather*, Mario Puzo sets up a classic trap: The murder of Sonny, it turns out, was contrived by his brother-in-law—the "no-good" who married his sister. Michael, as the new head of the family business, has to kill his brother-in-law to maintain structure and discipline in the business.

   This incident is portrayed not as revenge, but as a family cleansing. Puzo here feeds our naturally uneasy feelings about in-laws. He leaves the viewer with no choice. That's just the way it is, we conclude. This situation is exaggerated, of course, but it is not unusual for some family business members to feel that the only choice is to get rid of all in-laws.

3. *It is sometimes better to lie in a family business than to tell the whole truth.* Probably the finest moment in *The Godfather* is the last scene. It depicts

the best method of handling impossible conflict when there is no good choice. Just after Michael has his brother-in-law executed, Michael's sister confronts him. She accuses him of murdering her husband and calls him a cold, heartless person with no feelings for her children, who are now fatherless. To think that Michael, who had just become godfather to these children, would have their father killed, makes the act merciless. Talk about a tough management dilemma!

After the sister's tirade, Michael is left to face his wife, who launches into a similar tirade. Puzo does his finest work here, showing how to handle the most difficult kinds of confrontations in family businesses—the ones that threaten to destroy both the family and the business in one swoop.

Michael turns to his wife, slams his fist on the desk, looks into her eyes and says, "I thought we had an agreement in this family never to discuss business—never. Do you remember that agreement?" See how graciously he defuses this confrontation?

His wife answers, "Yes, but this is no ordinary circumstance."

After a long pause, Michael responds, "Well, in that case, I'll violate this sacred rule this one time, and I will discuss business. But only this one time. Never again. OK?"

And his wife says, "OK. Did you have our brother-in-law killed?"

Michael looks her straight in the eye and says, "No," firmly, emphatically, and convincingly.

The principle portrayed by Puzo here is that sometimes it is better to lie than to tell the whole truth when you own a family business. The entrepreneur plays by the rules when he wins and changes the rules when he loses so that he can win. It's not just doing things right in business, it's doing the right thing.

4. *The founder of the business possesses business instincts that can never be gained from books or schooling. It's his job to pass this knowledge on to the kids.* In his role as the godfather, Marlon Brando handles the difficult task of succession masterfully. The transition of Don Corleone from godfather to adviser and counselor to his son Michael, the new boss, echoes the role a board of directors or a trusted outside consultant would play in a family business. Michael has to reassign his former counselor, played by Robert Duvall, to make room for his father, the retired don.

The father constantly reminds Michael, for example, that the opposition would eventually seek to set up a "friendly" meeting. Even as his senility increases, the father continues to repeat, "If a member of the family approaches you about that initial meeting, he will be the one who betrays you. Remember that." Over the course of the movie, Puzo works in that advice repeatedly.

Years later, an associate approaches Michael to set up a so-called "friendly" meeting and is indeed someone about to betray him. Michael has to arrange the killing of this former friend to protect the business.

The transfer of critical knowledge from the senior to the junior generation is a crucial element of family business survival. It's the job of the senior person to be sure the junior person gets the message at all costs.*

I've taken four principles of family business and shown how brilliantly they were interwoven into this colorful movie. Rethink these principles as you consider the family business option and review *The Godfather.* They represent ideas that make up the prevailing wisdom about family businesses. Whether true or false, they have a strong impact because they are interwoven into our society.

5. *Every family business should have a "godfather."* This principle is not drawn from the movie but is still a sound practice. This "godfather" is a person who is trusted and respected by all the family and could serve as a mediator should that become necessary. He or she should be unbiased and have little or no vested interest in the company. The godfather can be a business acquaintance, friend, college professor or someone respected in the field. Bring this person into the picture right at the beginning and keep him informed. This is not the sort of person you find in the middle of a crisis. Professor John Ward plays this role in the Stew Leonard story outlined earlier in this chapter.

If you are lucky, you may never need a "godfather" to do more than settle minor disputes or serve as a sounding board for new ideas. If the worst comes to pass, though, and the business must be dissolved, this person may be the only one who can keep the pieces together long enough for the busi-

---

* At a recent CEO Club event in Manhattan, one of the lifetime members was asked a question during a new member introduction. His name is Rick Globus, and he and his twin brother, Steve, manage a well-known venture capital pool called The Globus Growth Group. Rick described himself as the long-haired flaky brother, as compared to his straighter, more numbers-oriented, shorter-haired twin. The question was, "How did you learn the venture capital business—did you go to business school?" Rick said, "Not really. I learned all I know from my dad, who started the business. Just hanging around the house taught me more than I learned any other way, including business school."

ness to regain its equilibrium and survive. Nothing lasts forever, but the business, if it survives at all, will probably outlive the closeness and trust the original family counted on as it was building the business.

■ The Guccis: Who's on First?

A real-life Italian family business is that of the Gucci family, whose members have probably spent more time rushing into court than the Corleones did trying to stay out. Creators of the finest in fashions, the Gucci family has been anything but harmonious. Three generations of bitter feuding pitted father against son, uncle against nephew, cousin against cousin. After more than 20 lawsuits, the empire has passed to Maurizio Gucci, the grandnephew of the founder, but he has ahead of him the daunting task of restoring the luster to the oversold Gucci name.

The company, founded in 1923 by Guccio Gucci, a leather goods craftsman whose initials form the firm's internationally recognized logo of interlocking Gs, emphasized Florentine quality and tight family control. After Mussolini invaded Ethiopia in 1935, the League of Nations sanctions cut Guccio off from his main source of leather. He designed a line of canvas luggage adorned with his initials and the family mark was born. The two Gs have been a golden goose ever since.

Of Guccio's three sons, only Aldo, the oldest, really jumped into the business. After his first visit to the United States, Aldo pursued overseas expansion, opening 180 stores abroad, which account for 82 percent of the parent company's sales. Aldo, in turn, brought his three sons, Giorgio, Paolo and Roberto, and his nephew Maurizio (who inherited his father Rodolfo's 50 percent of the shares) into the business.

In 1982, the family was irrevocably split. When Paolo proposed the marketing of inexpensive items under the Gucci name, he was ousted from the company during an explosive board meeting. Paolo sued the family for $13.3 million in the New York courts, claiming that Aldo, assisted by Roberto, Giorgio and Maurizio, had struck him with the tape recorder he had sneaked into the meeting. He more effectively alleged that his father, Aldo, had evaded U.S. taxes. Aldo was forced to admit his evasion and received a one-year jail sentence from the U.S. government. Meanwhile, nephew Maurizio used his 50 percent share to seize control of the company and oust Uncle Aldo. He brought in a new team of managers to help run the company professionally.

Maurizio's initial reign was short-lived. Aldo's other sons, Giorgio and Roberto, countersued, claiming Maurizio's shares were based on forged documents and also charging *him* with tax evasion. The Italian government, having had just about enough, stepped in, freezing Maurizio's shares and appointing Maria Martellini, a professor of economics from Milan's Bocconi school, to replace him as a state custodian. She told the family point-blank, according to a piece by Nancy Marx Better in *Manhattan, Inc.* magazine, "...for the sake of the Gucci operation, they should keep their own problems away from the company. Gucci is not a family business any more. It is not vital to have a family member working for the company." Under state-controlled management, the company expanded production, standardizing the quality of its stores and trimming its product line.

While in exile, Maurizio plotted. In late 1987, Morgan Stanley hooked him up with Investcorp, a Bahrain-based group that specializes in acquiring troubled companies and turning them around. Investcorp makes messy situations like the Guccis their business. Using Morgan Stanley as a conduit, Investcorp acquired the other Guccis' holdings and brought back Maurizio as chairman of the company.

One of Maurizio's first moves was to put his father's right-hand man, Dominico De Sole, in charge of the American operation. It is even rumored that on his deathbed Rodolfo made De Sole promise to take care of Maurizio, who is five years his junior. Another outside adviser brought in by Maurizio was Dawn Mello, former president of Bergdorf Goodman. Her responsibility was to create a new in-house design team to restore the luster to the faded Gucci name.

After years of feuding, Maurizio is finally heading the company, having vanquished the rest of the family, but his position is not yet secure. For one, he'll have to make sure his outside advisers, De Sole and Mello, don't start feuding themselves. Some people suggest, after all, that Maurizio brought in Mello to show De Sole who was boss. De Sole was not even invited to interview her. And then there's Investcorp hovering in the background, capable of selling the firm again to another private buyer, or forcing a public sale.

■ The Binghams of Louisville

As I mentioned earlier in this chapter, some family business decisions hurt the family and some hurt the business, but occasionally a situation develops that threatens to destroy both. The Gucci internecine struggle clearly destroyed the family, but the business has managed to survive. The Binghams of Louisville were not so lucky.

As many readers probably already know from the press reports of her story and the three books recounting it, Sarah "Sallie" Bingham used her stock to force the sale of the Bingham newspaper empire because she felt her ideas and her 15 percent of the companies were not being considered. Her parents had given her the stock, feeling strongly the company must be divided equally among the children. Had they given her something else of equal value, the company might have stayed in the family.

The Binghams repeatedly made that mistake, and it led over time to the downfall of the business and the dissolution of family ties.

According to David Leon Chandler's provocative book, *The Binghams of Louisville: The Dark History Behind One of America's Great Fortunes,* Barry Bingham began working on the papers as a police reporter in 1930 and became acting publisher when his father and owner of the papers, Robert Worth Bingham, was appointed ambassador to Great Britain. Upon Robert's death in 1937, Barry became publisher of the *Courier-Journal* and the *Louisville Times.* He also upgraded the Bingham radio station, eventually opened one of the first television stations, WHAS, and ran the profitable Standard Gravure printing company. By all accounts he was a fine (though autocratic) publisher; and under his direction the newspapers became a journalistic institution of the nation, taking the lead on a variety of liberal causes, such as civil rights, opposition to the Vietnam war and environmental concerns.

Barry and his wife, Richmond belle Mary Caperton, had five children. The firstborn, Worth, was carefully groomed for succession, violating the "don't put all your eggs in one basket" principle I discussed earlier with regard to the Corleones. Sure enough, Worth was killed in a freak accident when he was 34, leaving his unprepared younger brother, Barry, Jr., to run the company (youngest son Jonathan died at 21 of accidental electrocution). Barry, Jr. gave up the television career he had been planning and agreed to prepare himself to take over as editor and publisher of the newspapers. He succeeded his father as CEO after Barry, Sr. retired in 1971, retaining a position as chairman of the boards of the family companies.

During the 1960s and 1970s, the Bingham daughters, Eleanor and Sallie, left Louisville to pursue their own interests, as neither had ever been considered even as potential successors. Each daughter made a mark for herself, Eleanor producing television documentaries and Sallie winning awards for her fiction and book contracts. With such aptitude, Sallie might have made valuable contributions to the family business instead of becoming the agent of its destruction.

In the late 1970s, both daughters returned to Louisville—Eleanor to raise her children and Sallie to nurse the wounds of her two failed marriages. Their return prompted Barry, Sr. to make a fatal mistake. Fearing what he termed "the grandchildren syndrome," whereby the sheer number of third-generation owners splits the business apart, he made the two daughters voting members of the boards of the family companies. Going whole-hog against another vital principle, he also appointed his wife, Worth's widow and Junior's wife to the board. Conflict broke out almost immediately, with Barry Jr. accusing the board of Monday morning quarterbacking and board members, particularly the sisters, demanding more information and more control.

After Sallie began making public comments alleging sexism at the Bingham companies, her parents tried to mollify her by adding her to the newspaper staff as a book editor, at an entry-level salary. She and her sister continued to have sharp disagreements with Barry about the papers' political endorsements, editorials and operation.

In 1980, Barry, Jr. insisted that all board members sign a buy-back agreement stipulating that if they received an outside offer to sell their stock, the Bingham companies would have 60 days to match the offer. Sallie was the only member to refuse to sign. Three years later Barry, Jr. issued an ultimatum: Either the women left the board or he would resign. He had reached this point, he said, after consulting with family business adviser Leon Danco, who told him he needed a professional board of directors, not family members with no business experience. (Sound familiar?) Sallie refused to budge.

Barry, Jr. offered a compromise: He would turn over management of the companies to a group of nonfamily professional managers. Barry Sr. refused to allow it, saying that the companies might as well be sold if Binghams were not going to manage them. Finally, Sallie was voted off the boards in March of 1984. All the other women resigned and Sallie shocked the family by announcing that she would sell her stock to outside bidders.

In July, in an effort to end the family feud, Sallie offered to sell her 15 percent share to the family. This plan was soon derailed, however, when the family's investment bank appraised her shares at around $25 million, while her own private appraisers estimated their value at over $80 million. Accordingly, she resumed her plan to sell to outsiders.

In a countermove, Barry, Jr. offered to allow Eleanor, who was by this time also disgruntled, to run WHAS, the TV station, on the condition that she convince Sallie to sell at the family price. Eleanor eventually agreed, but only if the family could reach an agreement with Sallie on a price. Sallie dropped her price to $32 million; Barry, Jr. countered with a refusal to go above $26.3 million. At this point, Barry, Sr. stepped in to announce that he was selling all the companies to regain peace in the family and to ensure financial security for future generations. Sallie's share of the total sale came to about $82 million, with her stock worth more than twice what she had been offered by Barry, Jr.

The Bingham experience is unfortunately familiar. When gifts of stock are made to children, future battle lines are drawn between inactive shareholders and active family managers of the business. The natural tendency is for the passive shareholders to be intolerant of the business decisions made by the "insiders" and for the insiders to see the "outsiders" as parasites who don't know what they're talking about.

Many parents unwisely give equal shares of voting common stock to active and inactive children. Annual gifts of voting stock make tax sense but don't create a good long-term environment for the business. On the other hand, non-voting preferred and common shares for inactive children are not the answer, either, as children deprived of a voice in company affairs are at the mercy of those running the business. Instead, consider giving the child who won't be working in the business other assets.

Any family business owner determined to give voting stock to passive and active children must seriously consider establishing an outside board of directors. Without a board of directors that genuinely represents all shareholders— active and inactive—most families will not be able to resolve the mistrust and power issues such stock arrangements engender.

One final note: Whatever position you hold in your family's business, be wary of asking your lawyer to speak for you to other family members. Try to keep your family members communicating directly with each other. Once the lawyers start picking up the phones, the risk of family war escalates. Keep your lawyer abreast of developments and heed her advice, but keep her out of family discussions unless actual buying and selling are being considered.

■ Johnson versus Johnson

When dyslexic billionaire J. Seward Johnson signed virtually his entire $500 million estate over to his third wife in his last will, he set off a vicious court battle among his heirs. In her book *Johnson v. Johnson*, Barbara Goldsmith speculates that the heirs to the Johnson pharmaceutical fortune were fighting less over money than over the love they never had from their manipulative father. Goldsmith writes: "J. Seward Johnson's behavior toward his children—his patterns of rejection and divisiveness—ultimately led them into a courtroom seeking to find what they had never had from him: recognition, a sense of worthiness and a measure of a father's love. Perhaps restitution for this loss came to be equated with money."

In his final will, signed on April 14, 1983—just 39 days before his death— Johnson disinherited his children and even cut out a bequest to his favorite charity. The woman to whom he left his estate, Basia Piasecka Johnson, married him when she was 34 and he was 76. She was employed as a cook/chambermaid by his second wife, and they were married eight days after Johnson's divorce from his second wife was final.

The six Johnson children—Elaine, James, Mary Lea, J. Seward Jr., Diana and Jennifer—promptly contested the will. Their lawyers also noted that Johnson had established trusts in 1944 for his children worth roughly $600 million and claimed Johnson felt his children had enough money and had not done much with what they'd already been given. Both sets of lawyers vied with each other to expose the seamiest of the family scandals.

According to Goldsmith, the trial was the longest, the most sensational and the most expensive will contest in U.S. history. Two hundred and ten lawyers had a hand in the litigation, which ended in this settlement:

- To each child: $6.2 million after taxes, and an extra $8 million to Seward, Jr. for his lost executor and trusteeship fees.
- To Harbor Branch, Seward's favorite charity during his life: $20 million.
- To Basia: all charges of fraud, etc., dropped, and a $350 million bonus.
- Basia's lawyer, Nina Zagat: all charges of fraud, etc., dropped, plus $1.8 million before taxes.
- Lawyers' fees: around $24 million.
- The IRS: around $86 million in taxes.

The Johnson case is clearly the story of a family business run amok.

Although J. Seward Johnson was a passive, second-generation inheritor who left the running of Johnson & Johnson to his older brother, Robert "the General" Johnson, his life and the lives of his heirs were profoundly affected (even ruined) by the family business.

To accumulate his massive fortune, Seward sat back and watched his stock appreciate. By all accounts, he was an isolated, introverted, sickly child, partly because his dyslexia—a little-understood condition in those days—was so severe as to render him functionally illiterate. Remember when I pointed out that a strong parent has either very strong or very weak offspring. In the Johnson case, founder Robert Johnson had both, and Seward was the very weak one.

Seward was abandoned by his mother, who took off for England after a female friend of hers kidnapped him and held him for ten days in her Park Avenue apartment for sexual purposes until his older brother (the strong offspring) rescued him. Throughout his life, Seward displayed uncontrolled sexuality: Not only was he unfaithful to various wives, but he also molested his daughter Mary Lea from age nine to sixteen.

Johnson & Johnson is composed of 160 companies, marketing health care products in 150 countries, with $6.4 billion annually in sales as of Goldsmith's writing in 1987. The company became a source of tremendous unearned wealth for the children and grandchildren of the founders, Edward Mead and James Wood Johnson. Two years after its inception in 1883, older brother Robert invested his interest in another company in Johnson & Johnson. He soon replaced James as president of the company and concentrated on utilizing Joseph Lister's method of sterilization (Lister had identified airborne germs as a source of infection) to produce antiseptic surgical dressings.

When Robert died, his son Robert took over the business and became surrogate father to his younger brother Seward after their mother abandoned them. Certain themes run repeatedly through the story of this family business: domination by an older brother, sexism, secretiveness and an "image of purity and Christian piety concealing self-indulgent behavior," according to Goldsmith.

Seward was openly content to allow his brother to run the family business. He told his daughter Mary Lea, "You can't have two captains of a ship. My brother's the captain of Johnson & Johnson." He did parlay his love of boats and sailing into forays around the globe that convinced him to encourage the global expansion of the company that Robert undertook.

It was Seward's passivity, though, that allowed Robert to take the company all the way. He had Seward's complete loyalty and confidence and apparently recognized how valuable this cooperation was: "I think the most important decision was one my brother and I made jointly to develop confidence in each other. We felt the possibilities of this company were unlimited so long as we maintained this confidence in each other." The Binghams should have been so lucky.

For whatever psychological reasons, Seward never built this sort of relationship with his own children. Through mental and sexual abuse, he broke them down and discouraged them from entering the family business. The children of the first wife, Seward, Mary Lea, Diana and Elaine, lived at one point in a rat-infested garage attached to a chicken coup on the grounds of Merriewold, the family mansion.

From the children's testimony during the contesting of their father's will, it is clear that his final complete rejection of them shattered their dreams of being loved and accepted by him. Indeed, their attempt to make a scapegoat of Basia is further testimony to the resiliency of the hope abused children seem able to hold on to in the face of overwhelming evidence that they are not loved.

As Goldsmith wrote: "The legacy that Seward Johnson was to leave his children was one of abundant inherited wealth and nothing more—no work ethic, no stress on education, little religion."

In fairness to Seward, I should note his own childhood, fraught with neglect and abandonment, hardly prepared him to be anything but a rotten father. The Johnson family consistently used its vast wealth to cover up its problems, from Seward's dyslexia to his sexual profligacy, his childrens' suicide attempts and his marital problems. As long as the business ticked along under Robert's command and the dividends rolled in, family members could run wild.

The lesson of Johnson & Johnson should be taken to heart by any parent/owner of a family business or, for that matter, by any parent. It's a lesson on the nature of vacuums. If money is all you offer your children when their needs for values, education and moral support are not filled, they may think they're living a swell life, but they won't be.

W.K. Vanderbilt put it more succinctly: "Inherited wealth is a big handicap to happiness. It is as certain death to ambition as cocaine is to morality."

It's strange but true that people who are constituted to make a lot of money are also psychologically constituted not to enjoy it, and those able to enjoy it are usually not capable of making it. As J.D. Rockfeller, Jr., said, "I was born into it and there was nothing I could do about it. It was there, like air or food or any other element. The only question with wealth is what to do with it."

■ There's a Ford in Their Future

The first Ford (William) arrived in the United States from Ireland in 1832 and settled in what is now Dearborn, Michigan. He selected Dearbornville simply because it happened to be the first clearing along the forest route Indian tribes had been traversing between the Detroit River and Chicago. William Ford's dream was to farm his own land, a privilege denied him in the old country. He married Mary Litogot in 1861 and built their farm home in the midst of a forest.

Henry I

Henry Ford I was born in 1863. Actually, Henry was the second child born to the couple, as their first died at birth in 1862. This little baby became the world's greatest entrepreneur of his time.

As happens even today, Henry's father was appalled when his son rejected the possibility of working the family soil. "To the elder Ford, on his own land at last, free of the old country, the farm was liberating; to Henry Ford, bored and restless, it was like a prison."*

The Reckoning, David Halberstam (Morrow, 1986), p. 73.

One of the most traumatic events in the young Ford's life was the death of his mother when he was 12. The depth of his mourning manifested itself in many ways later in Henry's adult life. He cherished the lessons he ascribed to her.

In December of 1879, Henry Ford (age 17) left for Detroit, where he worked for a high-quality machine shop. As an apprentice, he became immersed in machinery, working among men who, like himself, thought only of the future applications of machines. He earned $2.50 a week, which left him $1 short of meeting his weekly living expenses. To make up the deficit, he repaired watches in the evening for a jewelry store.

To jump ahead a generation, Henry Ford's grandson, Henry II, who was a chip off the old block, ran the Ford empire for several decades. In a highly publicized divorce, Henry II's second wife was awarded, among other things, $5,000 a week for life for cut flowers in her home! When compared to the original founder (Henry I), the difference between $1 and the wealth created is like night and day.

After five years in Detroit, Henry was enticed back to the farm with an offer of 40 acres of timberland, a gift from his father to rescue his wayward son from the city and his damnable machines. Henry Ford took it because he momentarily needed security—he was about to marry Clara Bryant. As history shows, fathers like to bring their wayward children into the family business, and many of them resort to bribery to make it happen.

However, nothing convinced Henry more of his love of machines than the drudgery of being back on the farm. He continued to spend every spare minute tinkering and inventing. He experimented with the sawmill; he tried to invent a steam engine for a plow. Crude stationary gasoline engines had been developed, and he was sure a new world of gasoline-powered machines was about to arrive. He desperately wanted to be part of it, so he told his wife they were going back to Detroit. And Henry was the head of the house.

His father continued to worry about him, saying, "He just doesn't seem to settle down. I don't know what will become of him." How many fathers have said these exact words?

Henry's first partner was Alexander Malcolmson, the first of several early fortunate investors. (Malcolmson's bookkeeper, James Couzens, sold out his $2,500 initial investment to Ford in 1919 for $29 million.) However, Ford and Malcolmson split over the direction of the company. Malcolmson was for building fancy cars, the most popular of the times, while Henry wanted to build plain, sturdy cars for the multitudes.

Ford's theory of building automobiles was "to make one automobile just like another automobile; just as one pin is like another pin, or one match is like another match when they come from a factory." Henry wanted to make many cars at a low price. "Better and cheaper," he would say. "More of them, better and cheaper."*

The coming of the Model T in 1908 sent Ford's career skyrocketing. It ushered in the modern Industrial Age—an age that benefitted rather than exploited the common person.

Model Ts were built on an innovative creation of Henry Ford's that became the universal method for building automobiles: the assembly line. And as the mass production increased, Henry Ford *decreased* the price of his car from the initial $780 in 1910 to $360 in 1917. By 1920, the company was earning $6 million a month after taxes and sold as many cars as the rest of the manufacturers combined. It takes an unusual survivor with deep commitments and a clever mind to achieve this accomplishment in human history. To also think that this person can simultaneously be a great father or husband is like asking a great prizefighter to also be a great pianist. In some ways the skills needed to be a great entrepreneur are opposite those needed to be a compassionate, reasoning person, and Henry Ford was the world's greatest entrepreneur!

The dehumanization of the automobile manufacturing workplace because of the relentless speed of the assembly line created serious morale problems among the workers. The labor turnover rate at one point was 380 percent. In order to keep 400 men working, Ford had to hire more than 1,000. In keeping with Henry Ford's simplistic methods of problem solving, he shocked the entire industrial world by establishing his famous $5 per day pay plan for Ford assembly line workers, which doubled their existing rate of pay. It is an example of how entrepreneurs can go against the grain.

Henry Ford hated bookkeepers and accountants. In fact, while passing through an office filled with white-collar workers, he instructed an aide to fire the entire group, claiming, "They're not productive. They don't do any real work; they're parasites!"

Ford once told a noted historian, "A great business is really too big to be human."

Even an apparently minor detail demonstrated the power of King Henry in the Ford Motor Company: "Any color, so long as it's black." Into this environment came the heir-designate, Edsel Ford.

---

*The Reckoning, p. 78.

Edsel Ford

Edsel Ford was born in 1893, the only child of Henry and Clara Jane Bryant. He was a courteous and dutiful child, and displayed many of the engineering skills of his father.

After working for the company for six years, Edsel became president of the Ford Motor Company on December 31, 1918. He was 26 years old. His first responsibility as president was an important one. He was entrusted by his father to buy out all the other stockholders in the company, thereby making the company a true family business. After this reorganization in 1919, Edsel owned 40 percent of the shares. Edsel was a considerate and knowledgeable CEO. Unlike his father, he was patient with people and never abrupt.

In 1916, Edsel married a Detroit socialite, Eleanor Clay. It soon became apparent that Eleanor Clay Ford brought a new and powerful personality into the Ford family. She immediately began to move her husband "out of the loose smothering orbit of his parents, providing him with a context of his own, and it was Eleanor who helped Edsel to stand as a Ford in his own right."*

She was a blunt person who said what was on her mind. Edsel, on the other hand, was discreet, inhibited by a desire to be loving and caring, which severely debilitated him in dealing with his autocratic father. They had four children: Henry II (1917), Benson (1919), Josephine Clay (1923) and William Clay (1925).

Henry and only child Edsel had a close relationship while Edsel was growing up, and they both shared a love of machines and the successes that accrued to the family and the Ford Motor Company. Henry was very generous with money to Edsel, paying him an average of $3 million a year during the 1920s. However, as Henry had demonstrated so often during his career, unexpectedly pulling the rug out from under business associates was a common occurrence, and his beloved son was not immune to this inhuman exercise.

Henry believed Edsel was too weak to handle the pressure of dealing with the threats from business associates and competitors. In his mind, he thought he needed to prepare his son for this eventuality by toughening him up. The problem was that the methods he used eventually broke Edsel's spirit. To many observers, Edsel's early death at 49 could be attributed to a broken heart at the hands of a loving but terribly misguided father. Remember my comments about weak, strong, weak, strong.

There was constant tug-of-war between Edsel and Henry over modernizing the Ford products as well as their factory facilities. The more Edsel submitted,

*The Reckoning , p. 78.

the more his father hurt him, and the more the boy was wounded, the more submissive he became.

After Edsel's death in 1943, the Ford Motor Company was in dire straits. Had it not been the middle of World War II, with its U.S. government contracts, the company might very well have gone under. The government needed the production capability of Ford to build war materials, and it was the intervention of the nation's highest officials who innocently preserved the company for Henry II, who was serving in the Navy.

Eleanor Clay Ford

Eleanor had been a witness to the destructive power of the elder Ford, and the Rasputin-like Bennett in making her a premature widow. She now sensed her senile father-in-law was in danger of turning the company over to Bennett, thereby cheating her son Henry II out of his birthright.

Bennett's debilitating reputation was well known to the government officials whose war effort depended on Ford's survival, so when Eleanor and Clara (Henry's wife) joined forces, requesting that Henry II be granted orders back to Detroit to run Ford with his grandfather, they agreed.

Henry II returned reluctantly, for his Navy career had granted him a taste of personal freedom from the family. He was named vice president in December 1943, granting him titular power—and the power of blood—but unless his grandfather moved aside and Bennett left the company, he would never be able to take control. Again, Eleanor put her foot down and forced the issue. She threatened to sell her stock, 40 percent of the company inherited from Edsel, unless old Henry stepped aside in favor of his grandson. Henry's wife Clara supported her completely. They fought off the old man's excuses and delaying ploys. With the threat, and a sense that these women were intensely serious, Henry Ford finally, furiously, gave up, and Henry II took control. Eleanor Clay Ford reigned as the "Queen Mother" of the Ford royal family for 33 years following the death of her husband, until her death in 1976.

Henry II—Successor-Designate

Though there were four children born to Edsel and Eleanor Clay Ford— Henry II, Benson, Josephine Clay and William Clay, there was little doubt Henry II was the logical choice to lead the company. He was the oldest, and none of his siblings possessed his leadership qualities to challenge this transition.

Henry Ford II was an anomaly. He could spend hours carousing on the town with his friends, and the next morning he would be on the job bright-eyed and bushy-tailed. Woe to the drinking buddy who made the mistake of assuming that the shared intimacy of the previous night of revelry gained special privileges in Ford's office. He inherited his grandfather's unpredictability in handling close associates. When Henry II got turned off on someone, the suddenness of his actions in ending business relationships would leave the victim stunned and broken.

The Lee Iacocca incident is a perfect example of Henry's sharklike process, except that Iacocca may have been stunned, but, as history has proven, he was far from broken. The reasons for the dismissal of Lee Iacocca as president of Ford were strictly personal irritations that had little to do with his performance as president. In fact, Henry II had to threaten the board of directors, "It's either him or me," for Iacocca had made a lot of money for Ford.

Henry II was married three times and went through two ugly divorces that fueled the fires of tabloid journalism for several years.

When Henry II took over the ailing company in 1945, it prompted one observer to say, "The company is not only dying, but is already dead waiting for rigor mortis to set in. But Henry Ford hired the famous group, The Whiz Kids, and then took the company public. These actions helped Ford create one of America's great family businesses.

Henry II's turbulent life ended on September 29, 1987, from pneumonia. He had served as Ford's CEO from 1945 until October 1, 1979, and retired from the company as an officer and employee in 1982.

Henry II's Siblings

Benson Ford's career was bland and colorless, as he held responsible positions principally in the administrative part of the company. He died of a heart attack in July 1978.

William Clay Ford, the "kid brother," probably never had a chance to realize his full potential because of the timing of his older brother Henry's rise to power. He went to work for the company in 1949. He was chairman of the executive committee in 1978 and was elected vice chairman of the board of directors in 1980. Bill Ford's destiny was touched by the same dynamics that destroyed the Edsel. He spearheaded the marketing of a car to go head to head with GM's Cadillac, called the Continental.

One afternoon soon after the Continental was killed, Benson and William were visiting their mother. She asked them why they weren't doing more to help Henry. Bill looked at Benson and smiled bitterly. "Because he doesn't want us to," he said.

William Clay Ford currently owns the Detroit Lions football team.

The Fords of the Future

Not only are the Fords prolific in producing offspring, but they have a penchant for producing heirs interested in the automobile business.

Edsel Ford II (Henry II's son), 42, is a member of Ford's board of directors and executive director of the marketing staff. He has worked for the company since 1974 in several management capacities, just completing a hitch as general sales manager of the Lincoln-Mercury division. He has three sons, Henry III, Calvin and Stewart.

William Clay Ford, Jr., 33, is also a member of the board of directors. He joined the company in 1979 and has held several management positions at Ford. His most recent position was heavy truck engineering and manufacturing manager from July 1989 to March 1990, when he assumed his present position as director of business strategy for the Ford Automotive Group. He has two daughters, Eleanor and Alexandra.

Benson Ford, Jr., 41, joined the company in 1986 as a service management specialist, in parts and service. He currently is an accessories merchandising specialist in the same division.

Walter Buhl Ford III (son of Josephine Clay Ford), 47, joined the company in 1978 as program coordinator in the design center. He now is sales promotion coordinator, Lincoln-Mercury division. He has four children, Bridget, Lindsey, Wendy and Barbara.

The Final Family Business Lesson

It is more than 100 years since Henry I sold his first automobile for $200 and immediately used the money to build another one. The Ford Motor Company is currently one of the most successful corporations in the world, with revenues in the billions. Like the logo on Ford products, Ford family members in the business are still prominent.

The Ford family has not been immune to tragedy and conflict, but neither is any family. The unique message from the Fords is that their negative family processes did not destroy their family business. Even though many of the Ford clan led colorful and indulgent personal lives, the successful operation of the business was a priority to most of them.

APPENDIX

■

Resources

■ Accountants

Below is a list of accountants who can help you in all business-related matters.

Boston
Sanford N. Cooper
Managing Partner
Cooper & Company, P.C.
One Wall St.
Burlington, MA 01803
617/273-3550
617/273-2522 Fax

Alan S. Zelbow
Partner
Miller, Wachman & Co.
40 Broad St.
Boston, MA 02109-4317
617/338-6800
617/338-8485 Fax

Chicago
Allan Koltin
President
Practice Development Institute
410 N. Michigan Ave.
Chicago, IL 60611
312/245-1930
312/644-4423 Fax

Sam N. Oliva
Partner
Edwin C. Sigel, Ltd.
3400 W. Dundee Rd.
Northbrook, IL 60062
708/291-1333
708/291-1190 Fax

Dallas
Mark Lancaster
Partner
Deloitte & Touche
Lincoln Plaza
500 N. Akard St., #1400
Dallas, TX 75201-3302
214/720-8325
214/720-8450 Fax

Los Angeles
Melvin I. Poteshman
Managing Director
Levine, Cooper, Spiegel & Co.
11835 W. Olympic Blvd.
Los Angeles, CA 90064
310/477-7111
310/479-4323 Fax

Harvey Goldstein
Managing Partner
Singer, Lewak, Greenbaum &
Goldstein
10960 Wilshire Blvd.
Los Angeles, CA 90024
310/477-3924
310/478-6070 Fax

New York
Jay Trien
Managing Partner
Trien, Rosenberg, Felix,
Rosenberg, Barr & Weinberg
177 Madison Ave., PO Box 1982
Morristown, NJ 07962-1982
201/267-4200
201/984-9634 Fax

Bruce J. Strzelczyk
Partner
Arthur Andersen & Co.
1345 Ave. of the Americas
New York, NY 10105
212/708-8119
212/708-3630 Fax

Phil Zimmerman
Managing Partner
Paneth, Haber & Zimmerman
600 Third Ave.
New York, NY 10016
212/503-8888
212/370-3759 Fax

Pittsburgh
Lawrence F. Ranallo
Partner
Price Waterhouse
600 Grant St.
Pittsburgh, PA 15219
412/355-7714
412/391-0609 Fax

Washington, DC
Mr. Barry Schimel
Partner
Aronson, Fetridge, Weigle &
Schimel
6116 Executive Blvd., #500
Rockville, MD 20852
301/231-6200
301/231-7630 Fax

■ Advertising

Advertising Age
Crain Communications
740 N. Rush St.
Chicago, IL 60611
312/649-5200
800/678-2724

The leading newspaper serving the advertising industry. Presented in tabloid format, issues exceed 100 pages. This widely read and often-quoted weekly paper focuses on advertising in the broadest sense.

Adweek
ASM Communication
1515 Broadway
New York, NY 10036
212/536-5336
800/722-6658

Publishes five weekly regional editions that report on the advertising industry. Look in your local yellow pages or contact the publisher.

Bacon's Publicity Checker
Bacon's Information, Inc.
332 S. Michigan Ave., #900
Chicago, IL 60604
312/922-2400
800/621-0561

The finest comprehensive source of publicity information in the United States; used by most public relations firms. It is published annually; four seasonal supplements list magazines and daily and weekly newspapers in the United States and Canada. Listings include information on circulation, frequency, publication dates and types of publicity used ($250).

Gale Directory of Newspapers and Periodicals
835 Penobscot Building
Detroit, MI 48226
800/877-4253

The most comprehensive source of print media information (formerly *Ayers Directory of Publications*).

Internal Publications Directory
National Research Bureau
225 W. Wacker Dr., #2275
Chicago, IL 60606-1229
312/346-9097

An all-in-one directory of house organs. Many large companies have internal publications that publish useful outside material.

News USA, Inc.
4601 Eisenhower Ave.
Alexandria, VA 22304
703/461-9500
800/355-9500

An excellent method of reaching the 10,000 newspapers in the United States.

Standard Periodicals Directory
Oxbridge Communications
150 Fifth Ave., #302
New York, NY 10011
212/741-0231

This service offers 11 separate directories and gives advertising rates, specifications and circulation for publications, broadcast stations and other media.

Standard Rate and Data Service
2000 Clearwater Drive
Oak Brook, IL 60521-8806
708/574-6000
800/323-4588

An extensive source of both print and electronic media; it is widely used by major advertising agencies.

Ulrich's Directory of Periodicals
R.R. Bowker Company
121 Chanlon Rd.
New Providence, NJ 07974
908/464-6800

Available in most libraries. R.R. Bowker also supplies ISBN numbers for all listed publications.

■ Associations/Organizations

Many organizations benefit small businesses by providing business advice, making contacts and lobbying for favorable legislation.

American Management Association
135 W. 50th St.
New York, NY 10020
212/586-8100

The AMA Growing Companies Program sponsors classes in sales, marketing, planning, management and finance for small and midsize companies. Fees for individuals $160; company dues are $450.

Association of Collegiate Entrepreneurs
342 Madison Ave., #1104
New York, NY 10173
212/922-0837

A group of college-age entrepreneurs that was founded by Fran Jabara and headquartered out of Wichita State University. It holds an annual conference and publishes several newsletters. This is a temporary address, as the group is seeking a new home.

Nasir Ashemimry
Business Ship
One Alhambra Plaza, #1400
Coral Gables, FL 33134
305/445-8869

Business Kids
1300 I St., N.W., #1080E
Washington, DC 20005
202/408-0699

These groups service high school and young entrepreneurs; also do extensive work internationally, including in the Soviet Union. The group offers a package of books and tapes to teach the youth of the world to be entrepreneurs.

Dr. Joseph Mancuso, President
Chief Executive Officers Clubs
(CEO Clubs)
180 Varick St.—Penthouse
New York, NY 10014-4606
212/633-0060

An elite group of 350 CEOs who run businesses with more than $2 million in annual sales. Members are dedicated to improving the quality and profitability of their companies through shared experience and personal growth. Eight meetings a year are held in each of nine city locations: Boston, Chicago, Dallas, Los Angeles, New York, Pittsburgh, Portland, San Francisco and Washington, D.C. The organization also sponsors three-day national programs.

National Association for the Self-Employed
P.O. Box 612067
DFW Airport, TX 75261
800/232-6273

Self-employed members have access to a business consultant hotline. Group health and disability insurance augments the package.

National Association of Manufacturers
1331 Pennsylvania Ave., N.W.
Washington, DC 20004
202/637-3000

Members total 13,500; lobbies the government on behalf of manufacturers. Membership dues: $500 to $100,000.

Jack Faris, President
National Federation of Independent Business
Capitol Gallery East, #700
600 Maryland Ave., S.W.
Washington, DC 20024
202/554-9000

Polls its membership to determine lobbying positions and provides a strong voice for small business interests in Washington. Also publishes a newsletter, the *NFIB Mandate,* eight times per year.

John Galles, Executive Vice President
National Small Business United
1155 15th St., N.W., #710
Washington, DC 20005
202/293-8830

A lobbying group serving manufacturers, service businesses, retailers and wholesalers. They offer group health care plans through Mutual of Omaha.

John Satagaj
Small Business Legislative Council
1156 15th St., N.W., #510
Washington, DC 20005
202/639-8500

A coalition of trade and professional associations that is an effective lobby ing group.

Bill Williams
The Executive Committee (TEC)
5469 Kearny Villa Road, #101
San Diego, CA 92123
619/627-4050

An association of CEOs meeting in local units across the United States and overseas (Japan). They act as a board of directors for businesses. Meetings are held monthly and annual fees are more than $7,000.

Ralph V. Whitworth, President
United Shareholders Association
1667 K. St., N.W., #770
Washington, DC 20006
202/393-4600

A political group dedicated to representing shareholders' rights on Capitol Hill.

Young Entrepreneurs Organization
1010 N. Glebe Rd., #600
Arlington, VA 22201
703/527-4500

An outgrowth of ACE, founded by Verne Harnish.

Young Presidents Organization (YPO)
451 S. Becker Dr., #200
Irving, TX 75062
214/541-1044

An international group with strong local chapters. It has strict age requirements.

■ Banks

A close and sympathetic relationship with a commercial bank can be very helpful to a growing enterprise, not only in facilitating loans, but also in securing business advice.

American Bankers Association
1120 Connecticut Ave., N.W.
Washington, DC 20036
202/663-5000

Any information you might need on the status of the banking industry is available from this trade organization of about 14,000 members.

Bankers Systems, Inc.
P.O. Box 1457
St. Cloud, MN 56302
612/251-3060

Publishes the widely used Robert Morris Projection of Financial Statements form, for preparing financial statements in a business plan.

The Center for Entrepreneurial Management
180 Varick St.—Penthouse
New York, NY 10014-4606
212/633-0060

Publishes *How to Get a Business Loan Without Signing Your Life Away,* a book, a four-hour videotape and an audiotape program by Dr. Joseph R. Mancuso.

Executive Enterprises
22 W. 21st St.
New York, NY 10010
212/645-7880

Offers seminars and publications for the banking industry.

Independent Bankers Association
P.O. Box 267
1168 S. Main St.
Sauk Center, MN 56378
612/352-6546

Another good trade organization working with banks that help small businesses.

Robert Morris Associates
1650 Market St., #2300
Philadelphia, PA 19103
215/851-9100

The predominant training organization for commercial lenders. Provides valuable industry statistics and financial ratios.

R.L. Polk & Company
P.O. Box 305100
Nashville, TN 37230
615/889-3350

Publishes *Polk's Bank Directory,* the most complete source of bank information and bank listings ($170).

Sheshunoff Information Services
One Texas Center
505 Barton Springs Rd., #1100
Austin, TX 78704
512/472-2244

Veribanc offers information on banking to small business owners, but Sheshunoff offers similar and competitive information. Banks frequently use this service to uncover information on other banks. For $75 you can get a report analyzing your bank's capital strengths and income performance. With a credit card and a Federal Express account number (or a fax number) you can obtain invaluable in-depth data about any lender in one hour.

Veribanc
P.O. Box 461
Wakefield, MA 01880
617/245-8370

One of the best sources for checking up on the financial health of your bank.

■ Business Development Corporations and State Business Development Agencies

The purpose of business development corporations (BDCs) is to attract and retain businesses in their respective states, and thus increase employment. Although they sound like government agencies, BDCs are private organizations that operate within a state. Their shareholders are usually other private financial institutions located within the state, mainly savings banks and insurance companies, although industrial companies are sometimes investors.

Interest rates on BDC loans are usually from 2 to 4 percent above the prevailing prime rate. Some BDCs charge application and commitment fees, but they generally do not total more than 1½ percent of the loan. A prime advantage of BDC loans is the longer maturities available. A bank will rarely offer more than five years for a term loan; however, BDC loans have average maturities of between four and ten years.

Although most BDCs require collateral, many will accept second liens. Owners should be prepared to assign key man life insurance and to personally guarantee the loan if the business is closely held.

BDCs are lenders, not investors, and are usually not interested in equity positions in the business. However, a few, such as the New York Business Development Corporation, have formed small business investment company subsidiaries (SBICs). The SBIC will take equity positions, generally via subordinated debt with warrants (or a convertible feature), to round out a financing package.

BDCs are specifically designed to provide long-term capital to small businesses. For more information, contact your local chamber of commerce or the following:

National Association of State Development Agencies
750 First St., #710
Washington, DC 20002
202/898-1302

Contact for name and address of your state development agency.

■ Chamber of Commerce

The U.S. Chamber of Commerce is the largest volunteer business federation in the world. The individuals, companies, associations and chambers of commerce that it comprises represent all aspects of business in locations throughout the United States. The national headquarters has resources geared specifically to small enterprises.

U.S. Chamber of Commerce
Center for Small Business
1615 H St., N.W.
Washington, DC 20062
202/463-5503

The Center for Small Business provides issue reports as well as staffing for the Council of Small Business. It is actively involved in representing small business before the government. Small Business Programs, a part of the office of the Chamber of Commerce Relations, provides members with an information exchange, the *Small Business Update* and other publications.

U.S. Chamber of Commerce
North Central Regional Office
2000 Spring Rd., #600
Oak Brook, IL 60521
708/574-7918

Serves Illinois, Indiana, Kentucky, Michigan and Ohio.

U.S. Chamber of Commerce
Northeastern Regional Office
711 Third Ave., #1702
New York, NY 10017
212/370-1440

Serves Connecticut, Delaware, Maine, Massachusetts, New Jersey, New Hampshire, New York, Pennsylvania, Rhode Island and Vermont.

U.S. Chamber of Commerce
Southern Regional Office
13760 Noel Rd., #1150
Dallas, TX 75240
214/387-0404

Serves Arkansas, Louisiana, Missouri, New Mexico, Oklahoma and Texas.

U.S. Chamber of Commerce
Western Regional Office
500 Airport Blvd., #240
Burlingame, CA 94010-1988
415/348-4011

Serves Alaska, Arizona, California, Hawaii, Idaho, Nevada, Oregon, Utah and Washington.

■ Consultant Services

Consultants' Bookstore
Templeton Rd.
Fitzwilliam, NH 03447
603/585-6544

Provides free catalogs, a directory of executive recruiters and a monthly newsletter with inside information on the consulting industry.

Institute of Management Consultants
521 5th Ave., 35th Floor
New York, NY 10175
212/697-9693
800/221-2557

An association of management consulting firms composed of two firms that merged (IMC and ACME). Provides specialized professional management help and consulting directories.

Small Business Administration
409 Third St., S.W.
Washington, DC 20416
202/205-6600
800/827-5722 (hotline)

In addition to several good pamphlets on consulting and related subjects, the SBA offers two consulting services for small businesses: the Service Corps of Retired Executives (SCORE) and the Active Corps of Executives (ACE). Consult your local telephone directory for the regional SBA office nearest you, or contact:

Time-Place
460 Totten Pond Rd.
Waltham, MA 02154
617/890-4636

An on-line database of consulting professionals. Available through subscription database services and the American Society for Training and Development, it accepts advertising from consultants on database.

■ Directories of Telephone Numbers, Addresses and Zip Codes

National Address Information Center
U.S. Postal Service
6060 Primacy Pkwy, #101
Memphis, TN 38188-0001
800/238-3150, ext 680 outside of Tennessee
800/233-0453, ext 640 in Tennessee

U.S. Postal Service 1991 zip plus four directories and five-digit zip code directories are each just $12, a great value.

National Information Data Center
P.O. Box 2977
Washington, DC 20013
301/565-2539 (general information)
214/696-5156 (shipping information)

A two-volume zip code and post office directory ($30). They also sell telephone area code listings and maps. While this information is sometimes cheaper via the post office, NIDC is better organized than the Post Office.

Omnigraphics, Inc.
2500 Penobscott Building
Detroit, MI 48226
313/961-1340
800/234-1340

The telephone company now charges you for every long-distance information call. Using the *National Directory of Addresses and Telephone Numbers* saves money and time by listing most frequently called telephone numbers.

Superintendent of Documents
P.O. Box 371954
Pittsburgh, PA 15250-7954
202/783-3238

A complete directory of zip codes (about the size of the Manhattan yellow pages) is available from any U.S. post office. This is the cheapest source of zip code information ($15). Like all government agencies, they use voice mail and are almost impossible to deal with.

AT&T Consumer and Business Toll-Free Directory
800/426-8686

Has both yellow ($15) and white ($10) pages. Any telephone call made to a number in these directories is free.

■ Employee Stock Ownership Programs

There are many advantages available to entrepreneurs who elect to sell their business to their employees by using employee stock ownership programs (ESOPs). The new tax laws strengthen this option even further, although fewer than 10,000 companies have taken advantage of it to date. This program was created by lawyer-economist Louis O. Kelso and was sponsored by Russel B. Long, the Democratic senator from Louisiana.

Don Israel
Benefits Concepts, Inc.
101 Park Ave., 26th Floor
New York, NY 10178
212/682-9480

A group that is very active in establishing ESOPs on the East Coast.

Michael Keeling
ESOP Association
1726 M Street, N.W.
Washington, DC 20036
202/293-2971

An industry trade organization that is active in making ESOPs more attractive via legislation.

Patricia Hetter Kelso
Kelso Institute
505 Sansome St., #1005
San Francisco, CA 94111
415/788-7454

A nonprofit educational organization specializing in the employee stock ownership plan.

Carey Rosen
Karen Young
National Center for Employee Ownership
2201 Broadway, #807
Oakland, CA 94612
510/272-9461

A nonprofit association that provides information on ESOPs.

■ Family Business Resources

Dr. Leon Danco
The Center for Family Business
P.O. Box 24268
Cleveland, OH 44124

The dean of professional institutes, founded by the "grandfather" of family business, Dr. Leon Danco, and his wife Katy. The center has offered books, seminars and resources on the subject for more than 20 years.

Judy Green, Executive Director
The Family Firm Institute
12 Harris St.
Brookline, MA 02146
617/738-1591

The Family Firm Institute is an independent interdisciplinary organization dedicated to supporting practice and research in family-owned businesses. This trade association of practitioners in the field of family businesses provides a range of resources to answer the needs of today's family-run businesses, including a leading quarterly journal, *Family Business Review.* Its members are some of the better consultants in this field.

Frank Butrick, Managing Director
Independent Business Institute
3234 S. Cleveland-Massillon Rd.
Norton, OH 44203
216/825-8258

A major resource on family businesses, providing information and consulting services. It also publishes books and special reports for family firms.

Midwest Association of Family Business Owners
One South 280 Summit Court C
Oakbrook Terrace, IL 60181-3948
708/495-8900

A professional organization that helps to network family businesses.

John Messervey, Executive Director
National Family Business Council
60 Revere Dr., #500
Northbrook, IL 60062
708/295-1040

A private research and consulting group serving family businesses throughout the world. Its primary mission is to help resolve family issues directly affecting family businesses. It also is a resource for speakers on the subject.

■ Franchising

Franchising allows a manufacturer to conserve capital and to simultaneously establish a distribution system in the shortest possible time. Franchising exists in many industries: fast foods, motels, automobiles and parts, infrared
heating, business service, dry cleaning, home repair, health clubs, industrial
supplies, building products, schools, vending operations and so on. Although
franchise operations are not new, they have expanded greatly since the mid-
'70s. Millions of outlets now exist in all fields, accounting for more than $800
billion in annual sales.

A franchising operation is a legal contractual relationship between a franchisor (the company offering the franchise) and a franchisee (the individual
who will own the business). Usually the franchisor is obligated to maintain a
continuing interest in the business of the franchisee in such areas as site location, management training, financing, marketing, promotion and recordkeeping. In addition, the franchisor offers the use of a store motif, standardized
operating procedures, prescribed territory and a trade name. The franchisee, in
return, agrees to operate under the conditions set forth by the franchisor, to
buy all of his products from the franchisor and, in some cases, to make a capital investment in the business.

Entrepreneur
2392 Morse Ave.
Irvine, CA 92714
714/261-2325

The magazine publishes an annual franchising directory issue. The 1991
issue lists and rates 1,111 franchises.

Edward Kushell
The Franchise Consulting Group
1888 Century Park East, #1900
Los Angeles, CA 90067
310/552-2901

A fine group of experts.

Franchise Index/Profile: A Franchise Evaluation Process
Small Business Management Series, No. 35
Small Business Administration
409 Third Street, S.W.
Washington, DC 20416
800/827-5722

A guidebook for those interested in buying a franchise. It is also useful in familiarizing new franchisors with what prospective franchisees are looking for. Presents information through a series of questions to be asked of franchisors.

Franchising Opportunities Handbook, 1991 edition
Superintendent of Documents
P.O. Box 371954
Pittsburgh, PA 15250-7954

The most complete reference book of its kind. It gives information on the number of franchise outlets, length of time the franchise has been in business, start-up capital required and assistance given by franchisors ($16).

Donald Boroian, Chairman and CEO
Francorp
20200 Governors Dr.
Olympia Fields, IL 60461
708/481-2900

An excellent Chicago-based consulting organization. Their book, *The Franchise Advantage,* is excellent for franchisors. The Boroian/Mancuso book, *How To Buy and Manage a Franchise* (Simon & Schuster, 1993), is a best buy.

Information Press
728 Center St.
P.O. Box 550
Lewiston, NY 14092-0550
716/754-4669

Publishes a directory of about 5,000 franchises and information on Franchise News, Inc.

William Cherkasky
International Franchise Association
1350 New York Ave., N.W., #900
Washington, DC 20005
202/628-8000

Offers information and publications on franchising, including the quarterly *Franchising World* and my favorite, *The 21 Most Commonly Asked Questions About Franchising.*

Pilot Books
103 Cooper St.
Babylon, NY 11702
516/422-2225

Publishes a complete list of titles on franchising, including the *Directory of Franchising Organizations and Franchise Investigation* and *Contract Negotiation.*

■ Government Information

A great deal of information about small businesses is available from the federal government. However, getting that information is sometimes more difficult than tackling the problem it is intended to solve. Try contacting your state and city governments, your local chamber of commerce and various government associations. Your congressman's office is a good place to turn to when all else fails. Remember, your congressman works for you in Washington.

If you need information about selling your product overseas or about buying products from overseas markets, consult the New York City and Los Angeles yellow pages. These directories list most of the import-export offices of major companies.

General Services Administration
18th & F Sts., N.W.
Washington, DC 20405
202/501-1231
202/708-5804 (procurement information)

GSA arranges for the purchase of billions of dollars of items that civilian agencies need, such as computers, automobiles and office supplies. It provides two broad procurement services for small businesses: 1) specifics on what it is buying and whether individual small businesses might qualify as suppliers; 2) information and advice on selling to other federal agencies.

GSA provides its services through Business Service Centers in 13 regional offices (Atlanta, Boston, Chicago, Denver, Fort Worth, Houston, Kansas City, Los Angeles, New York, Philadelphia, San Francisco, Seattle and Washington, DC). For businesses located outside the 13 metropolitan areas with Business Service Centers, the GSA operates a Circuit Rider Program in which GSA counselors visit outlying cities periodically.

National Referral Service
Library of Congress
202/707-5522

A good starting point for most research. Conducts searches free of charge and handles most queries in less than five days. The Federal Information Center (202/707-5000) can direct you to the right government agency to get the information you need. There are 37 Federal Information Centers located throughout the United States. Their job is to assist the public in using the federal government as a source of information. To find a center near you, check the white pages of your telephone book under "U.S. Government."

Office of Innovation, Research and Technology
Small Business Administration
409 Third St., S.W.
8th Floor
Washington, DC 20416
202/205-6450

SBIR offers seed money grants to small businesses for research and development. Phase I grants range between $25,000 and $50,000. Phase II grants range between $250,000 and $500,000. Grants are administered by 11 government agencies.

Office of Business Liaison
U.S. Department of Commerce
Room 5898C
Washington, DC 20230
202/482-3176

Serves as liaison between the Commerce Department and the business community. Its free *Business Services Directory* is aimed at making the government more accessible to small businesses. Also available is the ROADMAP service, which provides information about government procurement, exporting, statistical sources, marketing and regulatory matters.

Diane Thompson
Procurement Automated Source System (PASS)
Procurement Assistance
Small Business Administration
409 Third St., S.W.
Washington, DC 20416
202/205-6600

SBA's Office of Procurement and Technical Assistance maintains capability profiles on small businesses interested in federal government procurement opportunities. Federal agencies and major prime contractors use PASS to identify the capabilities of individual small businesses. PASS participation forms are available from any SBA office or the above number.

Service Corps of Retired Executives (SCORE)
409 Third St., S.W.
Washington, DC 20416
202/205-6600
800/827-5722 Answer Desk

Part of the SBA. SCORE is an organization of retired businesspeople that provides actual or potential entrepreneurs with free advice. The answer desk provides information on all government agencies.

Small Business Administration
409 Third St., S.W.
Washington, DC 20416
202/205-6600
800/827-5722 SBA Hotline
202/205-6766 Small Business Development Center

Superintendent of Documents
P.O. Box 371954
Pittsburgh, PA 15250-7954
202/783-3238

One of the best sources of information around. For a small fee, you can get many booklets on business management and basics such as doing business with the federal government.

U.S. Department of Commerce
202/482-2000
800/872-8723

The Commerce Department's ITA will compile business profiles on your foreign competitors at a cost as low as $25.

■ Nongovernment Sources of Government Information

Government Procurement Assistance Center
1430 Davis Fort Rd., #12
Woodbridge, VA 22192
703/643-1072

A consulting firm that assists small businesses doing business with the government.

The Small Business Dealer's Guide to Selling to the Government
JTF, Inc.
P.O. Box 5521
Virginia Beach, VA 23455

An excellent source for the under $25,000 small business set-asides ($12).

Washington Researchers
2612 P. St., N.W.
Washington, DC 20007
202/333-3499

Founder Matthew Lesko has compiled a one-volume guide to "the largest source of information on earth," the United States government. Titled *Information USA*, this guide provides names, addresses and phone numbers for more than 3,000 government data experts as well as access to more than 1 million free and low-cost government publications (Penguin, $23).

■ Home-Based Businesses

Millions of Americans are finding that there is no place like home to work. It not only cuts down on commuting time, but it also offers financial incentives. Recent estimates indicate that there are more than 14 million home-based businesses in the United States. A number of associations, newsletters and books have sprung up to help the home-based entrepreneur.

Ed Simpson
Home Business News
12221 Beaver Pike
Jackson, OH 45640
614/988-2331

A bimonthly magazine for home-based entrepreneurs. Features articles on marketing, mail order and computers.

Georganne Fiumara
Mother's Home Business Network
P.O. Box 423
East Meadow, NY 11554
516/997-7394

A group of 5,000 members who publish a networking newsletter for mothers who work at home.

Betty Fifer
National Association for the Cottage Industry
P.O. Box 14850
Chicago, IL 60614
312/472-8116

Acts as an advocacy system for cottage workers. This 30,000-member group, founded in 1982, publishes a bimonthly newsletter, *Mind Your Own Business at Home.* Also publishes the *Kern Reports* on trends in home-based businesses and holds two meetings a year.

Cynthia Brower
National Association of Home-Based Businesses
10451 Mill Run Circle, #400
Owings Mills, MD 21117
410/363-3698

This 3,000-member group, founded in 1984, holds an annual meeting and offers a number of publications on operating a home-based business.

National Home Business Report
Barbara Brabec Productions
P.O. Box 2137
Naperville, IL 60567
(Requests for information by mail only)
708/717-0488

A quarterly newsletter that contains a wide range of information and advice on operating a home business. Also available is *Homemade Money* ($16.45 postpaid).

Starting and Managing a Business from Your Home
Department 146-R
Consumer Information Center
Pueblo, CO 81009

A 48-page booklet from SBA, which discusses the pluses and minuses of home-based businesses, including how to get started, recordkeeping, taxes and pertinent laws ($1.75).

■ Incorporating and Forming Partnerships

One of the first steps in setting up a business is to decide the form it will take: sole proprietorship, general partnership, limited partnership or corporation.

Corpex Bank Note Co., Inc.
1440 Fifth Ave.
Bayshore, NY 11706
800/221-8181
212/925-2400

If you want to purchase a corporate kit and stock certificates (including seal and bylaws) and don't want to pay a lawyer to do it for you, go directly to the source, the Corpex Bank Note Company.

Corporate Agents, Inc.
P.O. Box 1281
1013 Centre Rd.
Wilmington, DE 19805
800/877-4224
302/998-0598

A group of corporate register agents, will provide information on how to incorporate in Delaware.

Enterprise • Dearborn
520 N. Dearborn St.
Chicago, IL 60610
800/245-2665

How to Form Your Own Corporation without a Lawyer for under $75, by Ted Nicholas, is worthwhile reading for anyone considering incorporation. It is an excellent source of forms, books and quasilegal information. Dearborn Publishing can also provide forms for incorporation in any of the 50 states.

Lori M. Whitlock, General Manager
Delaware Business Incorporators
3422 Old Capitol Trail, #700
Wilmington, DE 19808
800/423-2993
302/996-5819

Can help you to incorporate in Delaware and to file to do business in your home state.

Nolo Press
950 Parker St.
Berkeley, CA 94710
510/549-1976
800/992-6656

The Partnership Book: How to Write Your Own Small Business Partnership Agreement, 4th edition (revised to cover new tax rules), was written by Dennis Clifford and Ralph Warner. Nolo Press also offers books for a few state incorporations. This is an excellent source of legal help for entrepreneurs.

■ Incubators

Incubators, which are most often run by nonprofit corporations, are designed to help start-ups get off the ground by providing low rent, business and financial advice (including advice on business plans and SBA loans), as well as secretarial and computer services. Studies show that start-ups in incubators fail only 50 percent of the time, compared with an 80 percent failure rate for businesses started on the outside.

Associations

Dinah Adkins
National Business Incubation Association
One President St.
Athens, OH 45701
614/593-4331

An industry trade association for incubators, the National Business Incubation Association is very effective in helping areas with high unemployment to create new business centers.

Miscellaneous Services

Office of Private Initiatives
Small Business Administration
409 Third St., S.W.
Washington, DC 20416
202/205-6600

Incubators Times, a quarterly newsletter published by SBA, keeps entrepreneurs up to date on the activities of business incubators around the United States.

■ Legal Services

Lawyers

Boston

Dennis O'Connor, Partner
O'Connor, Broude & Aronson
950 Winter St., #2300
Waltham, MA 02154
617/890-6600
617/890-9261 Fax

Chicago

Karen Carasik, Attorney
Much Shelist Freed, P.C.
200 N. LaSalle St., #2100
Chicago, IL 60601
312/621-1438
312/621-1750 Fax

Los Angeles

Barry A. Friedman
Friedman & Phillips
10920 Wilshire Blvd, #650
Los Angeles, CA 90024-6508
310/208-2889
310/824-1930 Fax

Tom L. Watters, President
Hart, Jakle & Watters
12400 Wilshire Blvd., #450
Los Angeles, CA 90025
310/826-5202
310/442-0181 Fax

New York

Roger Boyle, Partner
Boyle, Vogeler & Haimes
1270 Ave. of the Americas
New York, NY 10020
212/265-5100
212/757-3247 Fax

David McConoughey, Principal,
Wyatt, Gerber, Burke, & Badie
645 Madison Ave.
New York, NY 10022
212/826-0171
212/755-6256 Fax

Pittsburgh

Arthur Stroyd
Reed, Smith, Shaw & McClay
435 Sixth Ave.
Pittsburgh, PA 15219
412/288-3110
412/288-3063 Fax

Washington

Thomas McVey
Williams, Mollen
1401 16th St., N.W.
Washington, DC 20036
202/939-9620
202/462-3389 Fax

BOOKS UNLIMITED

Refunds within 14 days when accompanied

84991	Reg 1	8:29 pm 03/11/94

S MID CAREER ENTREP	1 @ 17.95	17.95
SUBTOTAL		17.95
TAX		1.08
TOTAL		19.03
CASH PAYMENT		20.00
CHANGE		.97

by register receipt. Mags. nonreturnable

Associations

American Arbitration Association
140 W. 51st St.
New York, NY 10020
212/484-4000

A good alternative to the court process. Used for a wide range of conflicts, including construction warranties, dissolution of partnerships, cost overruns and consumer complaints.

American Bar Association
750 N. Lake Shore Dr.
Chicago, IL 60611
312/988-5000

Maintains a legal referral service

■ Magazines of Value

Business Week
1221 Avenue of the Americas
New York, NY 10020
212/512-3896

Primarily covers big business, but it is widely read by small business.

The Entrepreneurial Manager's Newsletter
The Center for Entrepreneurial Management, Inc.
180 Varick St.—Penthouse
New York, NY 10014
212/633-0063

A monthly publication of CEM, a nonprofit membershp association of entrepreneurs.

Forbes
60 Fifth Ave.
New York, NY 10011
212/620-2200

One of the best-written general business magazines with a strong financial orientation and articles mostly about big business. The *Forbes 400* issue lists the richest Americans and the wealthiest families.

Fortune
Rockefeller Center
1271 Avenue of the Americas
New York, NY 10020
212/586-1212

A biweekly business magazine that competes with *Forbes* and *Business Week.*

Harvard Business Review
Soldiers Field
Boston, MA 02163
617/495-6800

Runs in-depth articles with strong academic analysis components. It is worth obtaining just for its index to other articles.

Inc.
38 Commercial Wharf
Boston, MA 02110
617/248-8000

The best and most successful magazine reaching the small business market.

Journal of Small Business Management
Bureau of Business Research
College of Business
West Virginia University
Morgantown, WV 26506

This is an academic journal that occasionally features practical articles.

Nation's Business
1615 H St., N.W.
Washington, DC 20062
202/463-5650

I consider this magazine, published by the U.S. Chamber of Commerce, to be one of the best general interest business magazines.

■ Mancuso's Favorite Business Newsletters

Jonathan Steinberg, Editor
America's Fastest Growing Companies
38 E. 29th St., 4th Floor
New York, NY 10016
212/689-2777
$245 yearly/48 pages/only on public companies

Eileen Pollack, Editor
Bankruptcy Law Letter
Warren, Gorham & Lamont
1 Penn Plaza, 40th Floor
New York, NY 10119
212/971-5216
publishes a wide variety of legal newsletters

Len Fox, Editor
Business and Acquisition Newsletter
Newsletters International Inc.
2600 S. Gessner Rd.
Houston, TX 77063
713/783-0100
monthly/$300

Business Law Update
Business Law Association
P.O. Box 247
Springdale, UT 84767
801/635-9817
monthly/$125/16 pgs./legal-ease information for CEOs

Gina Petrone, Editor
Business Opportunities Journal
1050 Rosecrans St., #8
San Diego, CA 92106
619/223-5661
monthly/$30/65 pgs.

James Kennedy, Editor
Consultants News
Kennedy Publications
Templeton Rd.
Fitzwilliam, NH 03447
603/585-2200
$158 per year

Chris Heide, Editor
Dartnell Sales and Marketing Newsletter Executive Report
4660 N. Ravenswood Ave.
Chicago, IL 60640
312/561-4000
26 issues/$170/8 pgs.

Katherine Helck, Editor
Direct Line
Direct Marketing Associates
11 W. 42nd St., 25th Floor
New York, NY 10036
212/768-7277
10 issues/only available to members

Linda Jorgensen, Editor
The Editorial Eye
EEI, Inc.
66 Canal Center Plaza, #200
Alexandria, VA 22314
703/683-0683
monthly/$87/12 pgs./free samples by request

Executive Wealth Advisory
National Institute of Business Management
P.O. Box 25288
Alexandria, VA 22314
703/706-5900
monthly/$100/investment strategies

Thomas Hitchings, Editor
Facts on File
Weekly World Digest
460 Park Ave. South
New York, NY 10016
212/683-2244
weekly/$640/20 pgs./offers condensed world news

Failed Bank and Thrift Litigation Reporter
Andrews Publications
1646 W. Chester Pike
Westtown, PA 19395
215/399-6600
$825 yearly/$450 for 6 months

Marsha Marlatt, Editor
Gift Retailers Assoc. & Manufacturers and Reps. Newsletter
1100-H Brandywine Blvd.
Zanesville, OH 43701
614/452-4541
4 issues/free to members/4 pgs.

Management Policies and Personal Law
Business Research Publications
817 Broadway, 3rd Floor
New York, NY 10003
212/673-4700
24 issues/$345/4 newsletters in one

Paul Swift, Editor
Newsletter on Newsletters
Hudson Associates
P.O. Box 311
Rhinebeck, NY 12572
914/876-2081
24 issues/$120/8 pgs.

Dan Kennedy
No B.S. Marketing Newsletter
Empire Communications
5818 N. 7th St., #103
Phoenix, AZ 58014
800/223-7180/FAX 602/269-3113
monthly/$100/newsletter on direct response marketing

Professional Selling Newsletter
Bureau of Business Practice
24 Rope Ferry Rd.
Waterford, CT 06386
203/442-4365
24 issues/$96/12 pgs./they offer 10,000 newsletters, but I like this one.

Helene Mandelbaum, Editor
Real Estate Investing Letter
861 Lafayette Road
Hampton, NH 03842
monthly/$96/10 pages

Stephanie Boyers, Editor
Small Business Bulletin
Small Business Service Bureau
554 Main St.
Worcester, MA 01608
508/756-3513
6 issues/16 pgs./primarily offers insurances for small businesses

Paul Kagan, Editor
Video Investor Newsletter
126 Clock Tower Place
Carmel, CA 93923
408/624-1536
monthly/$550/8 pgs.

■ Mergers and Acquisitions

Carl Wangman, Executive Director
Association for Corporate Growth
104 Wilmot Rd.
Deerfield, IL 60015
708/729-9070

A 22-chapter association concerned with mergers and acquisitions, including family businesses. This is an effective group for planning departments of larger businesses and business development officers.

Ray A. Sheeler, Principal
Business Valuation Services
3030 LBJ Fwy., #1650
Dallas, TX 75234
214/620-0400

Henry S. James, President
Corporate Finance Association of North California
344 Village Square
Orinda, CA 94563
510/254-9126

Two good sources for business valuation services.

Geneva Companies, Inc.
5 Park Plaza
Irvine, CA 92714
714/756-2200

Conducts seminars and provides information on buying and selling businesses. They also arrange for purchase or sale of family businesses. Has offices throughout the United States.

W.R. Stabbert
Institute of Certified Business Counselors
3485 W. First Ave.
Eugene, OR 97402
503/345-8064
415/945-8440

An association of business brokers that assists family enterprise expansion and development.

International Association of Merger and Acquisition Consultants
200 S. Frontage Dr., #103
Burr Ridge, IL 60521
708/323-0233

Specialists with expertise in medium-sized businesses. They maintain a database on all buyer-seller listings and publish a monthly newsletter.

Mergers and Acquisitions
M.L.R. Publishing
Rittenhouse Square
229 S. 18th St., 3rd Floor
Philadelphia, PA 19103
215/790-7000

A good resource magazine on buying or selling a business; covers emerging issues in the marketplace ($269/yr.).

■ Small Business Information

This category lists organizations designed to help small businesses as well as difficult-to-classify sources. Each source listed may be of value to your business, helping you to solve an immediate problem or to prevent a future problem.

Jan Zupnick
Entrepreneurship Institute
3592 Corporate Dr., #101
Columbus, OH 43231
614/895-1153

A nonprofit corporation that helps local communities pool their resources to help benefit small businesses. Their locally funded entrepreneurship forums provide information on state and local programs as well as networking opportunities.

Mark Stevens
15 Breckinridge Rd.
Chappaqua, NY 10514
914/238-3569

Mark Stevens is one of the best writers in the field of small business. His books are both helpful and informative

■ Venture Capital

Associations

National Association of Small Business Investment Companies (NASBIC)
1199 N. Fairfax St., #200
Alexandria, VA 22314
703/683-1601

An association of about 700 SBICs. It publishes a monthly newsletter and sponsors an annual conference on venture capital. A membership directory is available for a $1 handling charge (request in writing only).

National Venture Capital Association
1655 N. Fort Myer Dr., #700
Arlington, VA 22209
703/351-5267

A loose federation of about 200 venture capital sources. Publishes a membership directory ($15).

Western Association of Venture Capitalists
3000 Sand Hill Rd.,
Building 1, #190
Menlo Park, CA 94025
415/854-1322

Offers a directory of 130 members for $15

Angel Networks

Carroll Greathouse
International Venture Capital Institute, Inc.
P.O. Box 1333
Stamford, CT 06904
203/323-3143

Publishes a directory and a newsletter. There are about 1,200-plus venture capital firms in the United States and another dozen or so overseas.

International Venture Capital Institute
98 Hoyt St.
Stamford, CT 06910
203/323-3143

Lists 150 domestic and international venture capital clubs.

National Association of Investment Companies
1111 14th St., N.W., #700
Washington, DC 20005
202/289-4336

Publishes a directory of 150 member venture capital firms, mostly SBICs ($3.65).

Seed Capital Network, Inc.
8905 Kingston Pike, #12
Knoxville, TN 37923
615/693-2091

Has about 600 members in the United States.

Investment Division
Small Business Administration
409 Third St., S.W.
Washington, DC 20416
202/205-6600

Keeps a directory of all operating SBICs, which is updated every six months. Free

Technology Capital Network
MIT Enterprise Forum
201 Vassar St. W., #59
Cambridge, MA 02139
617/253-2337

A nonprofit corporation. This unique service matches entrepreneurs seeking capital with venture capital sources. Investors register for one year for $200. Entrepreneurs register for six months for $100. A faculty member of the University of New Hampshire, Bill Wetzel, knows of other similar services across the country. In fact, he is assisting nine other regional centers to become "angel" networks

A. David Silver
ADS Financial Services, Inc.
524 Camino del Monte Sol
Santa Fe, NM 87501
505/983-1769

David Silver claims to have raised more capital than anyone in the world. His Silver Press is a wonderful source of books and information, including who's who in venture capital.

Publications

Venture Economics, Inc.
1180 Raymond Blvd.
Newark, NJ 07102
201/622-4500

Stanley Pratt's *Guide to Venture Capital Sources* is the most valuable venture capital guide available today. His firm, Venture Economics (formerly Capital Publishing), also publishes a valuable venture capital and leveraged buyout newsletter.

■ Women Entrepreneurs

Women are emerging as a major force in the entrepreneurial world, and organizations and publications are springing up to help them.

Rosalind Paaswell
American Woman's Economic Development Corporation
71 Vanderbilt Ave., #320
New York, NY 10169
212/688-1900

Serves 500 active clients; fees are adjusted based on service provided and ability to pay. Services include training, individual counseling, networking seminars and an annual conference.

Lydia Lewis
Committee of 200
625 N. Michigan Ave., #500
Chicago, IL 60606
312/751-3477

A 200-member network of high-powered entrepreneurial and corporate women. Services offered include spring and fall conferences, a newsletter and regional meetings.

National Association of Women Business Owners
1377 K St., N.W. #637
Washington, DC 20005
301/608-2590

An excellent networking group, with 4,500 members. Membership is $100.

Kay Gudmestad
WomenVenture
2324 University Ave. West, #200
St. Paul, MN 55114
612/646-3808

Formed in 1989. Offers four major service areas: business development, initiatives for low-income entrepreneurs, career services and union apprenticeship training programs in the building trades.

Index

■ ■ ■ ■ ■ ■ ■ ■ ■ ■ ■ ■ ■ ■ ■ ■ ■ ■ ■ ■